SEASONAL PATCHWORK & QUILTING

✢

Colette Wolff

Meredith® Press

New York, N.Y.

Dear Quilter:

Thank you for selecting *Seasonal Patchwork & Quilting,* the fourth title in our annual quilting series. We know you'll enjoy this inviting collection of patchwork, quilting, and appliqué projects that were designed to reflect the seasons of the year in color, fabric, and theme.

With average sewing skills and the expert instructions of talented needleworker Colette Wolff, you can create the many appealing items for giving or keeping that were inspired by the colors and motifs of the changing seasons. The projects range from small flowers to full-size bedquilts. There are table toppers and wall hangings, dolls, holiday treats, and wearables too. *Seasonal Patchwork & Quilting* is truly a book for all seasons, with enough projects to keep your hands busy all year round.

We at Meredith Press are pleased to bring you high-quality craft books like this one. Our books offer a range of projects for every skill level and a variety of designs and uses to please every crafter. Large color photographs of the finished projects, accurate step-by-step instructions, and clear, readable charts, diagrams, and patterns are features found in all Meredith Press books.

We hope you'll have many enjoyable hours with *Seasonal Patchwork & Quilting,* and that you'll look forward to other books from Meredith Press.

Sincerely,

Barbara S. Machtiger
Editorial Project Manager

For Meredith® Press:

Director: Elizabeth P. Rice
Project Manager: Barbara S. Machtiger
Project Editor: Sydne Matus
Production Manager: Bill Rose
Design: Remo Cosentino/Bookgraphics
Photography: Schecter Lee
Illustrations: Colette Wolff

Distributed by Meredith Corporation,
Des Moines, Iowa.

ISBN: 0-696-02345-8

Library of Congress
Catalog Card Number: 90-062528

Printed in the United States of America

10 9 8 7 6 5 4 3 2 1

DEDICATION
To the memory of Maggie Ramsey,
a true and generous colleague.

Acknowledgments

To Stephanie Dell'Olio of Marcus Brothers Textiles, who patiently assembled the Christmas prints and antique reproduction fabrics from the Marcus Brothers line that I chose for the Fall and Winter projects in this book. To Priscilla Miller of Concord Fabrics, who opened the Concord showroom and cut the pastel florals and solids that I selected for the quilts of Spring. To Donna Wilder of Fairfield Processing Corporation, who is always there for authors in need of batting and stuffing.

To Karen Bray of Walnut Creek, California, for allowing me to adapt the machine-appliqué method described in her book *Machine Appliqué* to the construction of the "Choristers" panel.

To Alma Gallivan of Miami, Florida, for her meticulous and caring quilting of "Tying the Knot"; to Mrs. Lillian Johnson of Argyle, Wisconsin, who quilted the Sunbonnets so beautifully; and to Marie Wilson, who gathered yo-yos, pieced geese, tied knots, and makes friendship an adventure.

To Bonnie Askowitz for finding Alma, to Almuth Palinkas for her taste in fabrics, to Norma Ellman for the right word when needed, and to Agnes Birnbaum for everything.

Contents

Introduction

This is a book of original sewing projects, related by theme to seasonal headings, that utilize a variety of patchwork and quilting techniques. The projects were designed to be decorative but practical, to integrate construction methods and materials with function, and to be worth the time they will take you to make.

A few of the projects qualify as quick and easy, a few are destined to be heirlooms, some have challenging aspects, but all are within the capabilities of anyone who enjoys a stitchery adventure, who can machine-sew a steady seam, handle a needle with moderate dexterity, and follow instructions.

How to Use This Book

After you've leafed through these pages looking at the pictures and decided on a project that you want to make, read the instructions thoroughly. In this section, read the general information about tools and equipment, materials, and basic techniques. Scan the special terms and techniques information for reference as a particular instruction may require.

When you've gathered the specified materials, place the book, opened to the directions you'll be following, where it will be visible when needed. Take the time to execute each step carefully and thoroughly. Good craftsmanship is the essence of satisfaction as you work and a source of the pride you'll feel in a project that's beautifully finished.

TOOLS AND EQUIPMENT

Under the heading Materials, there's a list of the fabrics, notions, and other items required for each project, but that list doesn't include the basic tools and equipment you're expected to have on hand:

- a sewing machine with zigzag capabilities, a zipper/cording foot, and a foot with a grooved base for satin stitching
- a steam iron and padded ironing board
- paper-cutting scissors, fabric-cutting scissors, and small embroidery-type scissors
- straight pins, preferably with easy-to-spot ball or flower heads, and safety pins
- an assortment of hand-sewing needles
- a thimble
- a tube-turning device
- white paper, graph paper, tracing paper, and cardboard
- an X-acto knife
- cellophane and masking tape
- white glue
- a steel-edged ruler, yardstick, tape measure, compass, and protractor
- felt-tip pens and pencils
- an assortment of fabric markers such as dressmaker's colored pencils, thin-line chalk markers, and artist's pencils in several colors
- a pencil sharpener
- paper and fabric erasers
- a quilting frame and/or a quilting hoop

Tools that are helpful but not essential include a rotary cutter and mat, quilter's clear plastic grid-marked rulers, clear template plastic, a grid-marked cutting board, Clover tapemakers, and an embroidery hoop.

ASSEMBLING THE MATERIALS FOR A PROJECT

With few exceptions, you should be able to find the materials required for the projects in this book at fabric and quilting shops, sewing centers, and variety stores in your area. Mail order is another source. The dowels required for several projects are available at hardware stores and lumber yards. Earmuffs are a seasonal item and you can get the wire for yo-yo flowers from a local florist.

Fabric requirements are closely estimated, something to keep in mind if you're worried about possible mistakes. If fabric yardage is specified and width isn't, either a 36" or 45" width will do. Because cotton has adaptability characteristics absent in cotton/polyester fabrics, use only 100% cotton fabrics when that's indicated.

Some of the fabrics I used were supplied by the manufacturers credited in the front of the book, fabrics you may find in stock at a local shop. Other fabrics I either had or bought, and several were contributed by friends. However, my fabric color choices are guides, not decrees. Personalize the projects you make from this book with colors that reflect your preferences.

Before you start a project, *launder the washable fabric you intend to use!* With that precaution, you'll never be horrified by shrinkage or bleeding color when it's too late.

BASIC TECHNIQUES

The step-by-step instructions for each project exclude fundamental procedures that you're expected to know how to perform without further explanation. For the record, a quick review:

"Make copies of the patterns" means photocopying at your local copy shop or tracing by hand over the lines that show through paper placed on top of the page with the patterns. For working purposes, **patterns** are cut from sturdy paper and **templates** are cut from cardboard or plastic. When you need to cut only one or two pieces of fabric from a pattern, paper will serve nicely, but if you're cutting many pieces, you'll need to trace around material that won't disintegrate around the edges. To make templates, glue your paper copy to sturdy cardboard or trace the pattern onto clear template plastic before cutting out. (**HINT:** Sandpaper stapled to one side of a template prevents slippage when you're tracing its outline onto fabric.) Always include sewing notations (●'s, ○'s, ▼'s, straight-of-fabric arrows, etc.) and descriptive labels on patterns and templates, and back them up with reference copies just in case. If you anticipate repeating a project, make templates even if paper patterns are all that's required for one.

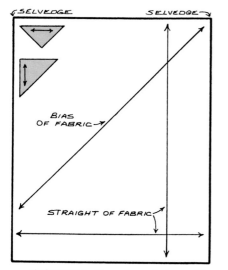

FIGURE 1. Two templates with straight-of-grain markings matched to the straight grain of the fabric.

Whether you're cutting paper, cardboard, or fabric, cut out the fabric pattern piece following the traced outline exactly. The **trace and cut** direction in this book means (1) tracing the exact outline of a pattern or template onto fabric with the pin-sharp point of a pencil tucked up against the edge of the pattern or template and, except for appliqué, (2) cutting the fabric exactly on that outline. Appliqué outlines are traced on the right side of the fabric; otherwise outlines are usually traced on the fabric's wrong side.

Before tracing or measuring and cutting, **square the fabric** by tugging it across the bias to return the crosswise and lengthwise threads of the weave to true 90° alignment. Unless you need to follow or frame the fabric's pattern attractively, match the straight-of-fabric arrows on a pattern or template to the straight grain of the fabric (see Figure 1). Transfer any notations (●'s, ○'s, ▼'s) to the fabric. Sewing notations of any kind, cutting lines, seamlines, quilting lines, and other marks, should *never* show on finished work! Before using, test the removability of markers on fabric scraps.

Except when following or framing the fabric's pattern attractively, align your ruler with a thread of the fabric when measuring and tracing straight lines prior to cutting to a specified size. You can make perfectly straight cuts without tracing by using a rotary cutter and a quilter's gridded ruler. If you want to be sure that corners are 90° angles, use a protractor or the corner of something you know is square, like a piece of paper.

Unless hand sewing is specified, machine sewing is used to construct the projects in this book. When **sewing** two pieces of fabric together, match the edges to be joined and stitch an unwavering seam that follows those edges by a specified distance. The distance between the seam and the edge of the fabric is called the **seam allowance**. In this book, the width of the seam allowance, usually ¼" but occasionally ½", is specified in the directions and included in the cutting dimensions. On patterns, seamlines are indicated by thin lines inside the heavier outline of the shape.

The edges of pieces to be joined, particularly when lengthy, are pinned together before sewing, and the pins are removed in front of the machine's presser foot. Sometimes **basting** is more efficient than pinning. Loose stitching sewn by hand or machine, basting is removed after final seaming unless the basting is confined within a seam allowance where it can remain hidden.

For general machine sewing, allow the fabric you're stitching to be moved under the presser foot by the action of the machine, especially if the edges being sewn are cut on the bias. Seams either travel from one edge of the fabric to another or start and stop somewhere within the fabric, in which case the threads must be secured or they'll pull out. To secure, you can (1) temporarily set your stitch length at 0 and stitch in place, or (2) backstitch for ¼" to ½", or (3) cut the threads, remove the fabric from the machine, pull the top thread through to the back and knot it to the bobbin thread.

When directed to "clip the curving seam allowance before turning right side out," cut across the seam allowance almost up to, but *never* through, the stitching. To turn right side out without pull marks, steep curves require more clips than slight curves.

If a fabric somehow acquires little pleats during seaming, unpick the stitches and **ease** the pleats out when you resew. Easing means adapting slack fabric to taut fabric along a certain stretch of seam by catching a tiny amount of slack into each stitch and steam-pressing smooth.

Set up your ironing board near your sewing machine so that you can **press** constantly as you work. When directed to press seam allowances closed, turn both seam allowances in one direction over the darker of the adjoining fabrics. For piecing, press matching seam allowances of adjoining rows in opposite directions to prevent clumping. Opened seam allowances are turned in opposite directions. Press on both sides of the seamed fabric, nosing over the seam in front to open it completely. Don't slide the iron over piecework seam allowances or they'll ruffle up; pick up the iron and set it down. Steam-press out-of-shape work-in-progress to straighten, flatten, and smooth; block finished work with more steam.

To preserve and enhance the dimensionality of appliqué and embroidery, steam-press right side down on an ironing board with extra padding (several towels or a piece of blanket). Never press work, like the quilts in the Spring section or the "Choristers" Christmas banner, that has been decoratively hand- or machine-quilted.

In these instructions, I use the term **tack** to mean connect or attach with appropriate stitching, usually by hand.

Special Terms and Techniques

Many of the projects in this book share special techniques that are listed alphabetically and explained in further detail below:

APPLIQUÉ

To apply cutouts of fabric, called appliqués, to another fabric, experienced appliquérs can choose from numerous methods. Those that follow are the methods I used to appliqué the projects in this book.

To **hand-appliqué** the Spring, Summer, Fall, and Winter panels and the "Tying the Knot" and Sunbonnet quilts, I alternated between three methods of preparing appliqués for stitching:

1. For appliqués with simple outlines and long edges, trace the outline of the appliqué onto the right side of the fabric, cut it out ⅛" to ¼" outside the traced outline and then, finger-creasing between thumbnail and forefinger, turn its seam allowance to the back, situating the traced outline exactly on the fold.

2. For most other appliqués, trace the outline of the appliqué onto the wrong side of the fabric and cut it out ⅛" to ¼" outside the outline. Then, working on a small surface padded with two layers of felt, place the template over the back of the appliqué, matching outlines, and trace around it with a large, blunt tapestry needle, pressing heavily to score the fabric as if it were paper so that, on the right side, the appliqué's seam allowance will turn under on the scored imprint.

To turn smoothly, the seam allowances at inside curves must be clipped almost to the fold (the deeper the curve, the more frequent the clips), and inside angles need clipping right up to the fold. After preparation, I pin appliqués to the foundation fabric, either matching the appliqué to an outline traced on the foundation or locating it by eye. I seldom baste.

I blindstitch appliqués with tiny stitches spaced ⅛" apart, closer for small shapes and convoluted outlines. With the tip of the needle, I shove seam allowances underneath and tease edges into smoothness just before stitching. I trim seam allowances at the sides and tip of a point and stitch very closely, at inside angles as well, to contain straying threads. (HINT: If pins continually catch sewing thread, pin from underneath.)

3. To prepare circles, such as the flower centers in "Tying the Knot," the balloons in Sunbonnet Sue, and the green apples in the Summer panel, for each appliqué trace the template's outline onto thin cardboard and cut out. Cut a circle of fabric ¼" larger than the template and, after sewing a line of running stitches within the ¼" enlargement, gather the fabric tightly around the cardboard circle. With the cardboard inside, blindstitch the appliqué to the foundation, cut away the foundation fabric behind the appliquéd circle, and remove the cardboard.

Cut out the fabric behind an appliqué when color shadows through and when the fabric behind adds an unwanted layer to quilt through. For hand appliqué, blend the color of the sewing thread with the color of the appliqué, not the foundation.

For the sweatshirt and the "Choristers" panel, appliqués are attached by machine stitching. To **machine-appliqué**, cut appliqués without seam allowances and sew to the background with satin stitching that zigzags over the cut edges. The satin stitching creates a visible outline of thread around the appliqué.

BINDING

Many of the projects in this book have edges that are sewn and wrapped with a strip of narrow fabric called binding. With the exception of the wallet, which must be bias-bound, all of these projects have straight sides and can be bound with either straight-cut or bias-cut strips, as preferred. For each project, the amount of binding fabric specified is enough to cut the required number of strips in either direction.

To withstand wear and abuse, all bindings are doubled. After cutting, strips are pieced to a continuous length specified for each project. The binding is then folded in half lengthwise, right side out, and pressed. Starting a short distance from a corner or at an inconspicuous place, align the cut edges of the binding with the raw edges of the item and machine-stitch. Then turn the binding smoothly over all these edges to the other side of the item and blindstitch to the fabric underneath, just covering the machined seam. Around corners, the binding is mitered, as illustrated in Figure 2, and secured with stitches. The ends of the binding are overlapped, with the seam allowance of the end on top turned underneath and secured with stitches. Except for the "Wild Goose Memories" comforter, bindings are tight and firm when finished. Although soft, the comforter's binding is filled to its limits, a requirement for good binding.

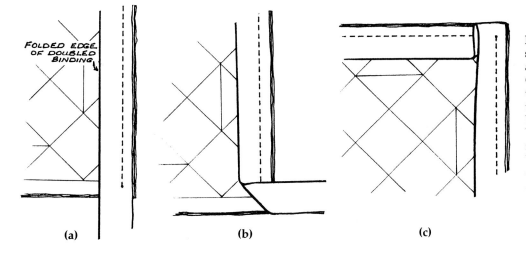

FOLDED EDGE OF DOUBLED BINDING

(a)   (b)   (c)

FIGURE 2. To miter a corner: (a) stop stitching the binding a seam allowance width from the corner; (b) turn the binding away from the quilt, making a 45° angle at the quilt's corner with the binding; (c) turn the binding back over itself, folding it to match its own edge; align the binding's edge with the next side of the quilt and resume stitching at the seam allowance point.

BLIND STITCHING

The blind stitch is used to attach the folded edge of appliqués and the folded edge of binding to the fabric underneath. Hand-sewn with single thread, it is invisible when each stitch picks up two to four threads of the fabric on the fold, disappears directly into the fabric underneath, and is pulled taut (see Figure 3).

(a)   (b)

FIGURE 3. (a) Blindstitching from the front where mini-stitches barely show and (b) the reverse side where the thread shows as it travels forward.

EDGE STITCHING

Machine stitching sewn from the front within ⅛" of the folded edge it follows, edge stitching attaches pockets, zippers, a waistband, and replaces handwork to secure a binding for some of the projects in this book. Another term, **topstitching**, describes visible machine seaming, usually decorative (like the satin stitching on Fall's tablecloth), laid down ¼" or more from the edge it follows. The word *topstitching* is often used when *edge stitching* is meant.

Threads at the ends of edgestitched and topstitched seams are tied to secure. To prevent knots from working out, bury the ends: after tying the threads, insert the threads into a needle; at the final stitch, run the needle under the top layer of fabric, bring it out half-a-needle's length away, and cut the threads where they emerge.

ENLARGING

The patterns for some of the projects in this book couldn't be printed full-size, so they appear reduced, superimposed with a grid of lines. To enlarge a pattern to the size needed to make the project, reproduce the grid on a larger sheet of paper but space the lines as the scale in the book specifies. For example, if the scale indicates that "1 square = 1 square inch," draw lines 1" apart. (HINT: Tape sheets of graph paper together and draw over selected lines.)

Starting at the upper left-hand corner, number the horizontal and vertical lines on both grids. Working one square at a time, duplicate the pattern's outline but stretch it to fit the enlarged square, gauging the proportions between outline and grid lines by eye. Continue square by square until the pattern's outline is complete.

LADDER STITCHING

After the ring pillow, the dolls, and the spin drops are stuffed, the edges of the stuffing openings are pulled together and closed with invisible hand stitching called ladder stitching (see Figure 4). Ladder stitching is also used to appliqué. For closing openings, doubled thread is necessary; for appliqué, use single thread.

FIGURE 4. To close an opening with ladder stitching, (a) take stitches through the folds, moving directly across the opening from one side to the other; (b) pull the thread taut and continue.

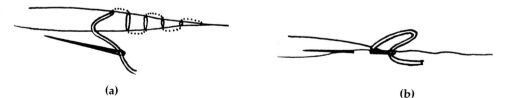

(a)   (b)

PIECING

The fabric used for projects as diverse as the portfolio, the tea cozy, and the comforter is constructed from smaller pieces of fabric machine-sewn together following a design. To finish flat with the dimensions and shape required for the project, every piece of fabric must be accurately cut and sewn. For precise seaming, create a seam-allowance guide by sticking several layers of masking tape to the bed of your sewing machine with the edge a seam allowance distance from the needle.

While working, avoid mistakes by arranging the cut pieces and sewn units next to each other as they will look when finally pieced together. When joining two rows of patches, connect the seams that need to match with a pin so that, after sewing, the seams will meet and cross exactly.

QUILTING

The lining, the batting, and the top of the bride's quilt and the Sunbonnet quilts are sewn together with hand stitching that indents a design into the padded textile. Since **hand quilting** options are numerous and books have been written about the technique, the explanation that follows is necessarily general.

After *lightly* marking the top with quilting lines as specified in the instructions, stack the lining, batting, and top in that order, carefully smoothing and aligning each layer. Baste the layers together with large, loose stitches, making seams that start in the center, move out to the edges, and finally crisscross the surface about 6″ apart. Put the basted quilt into a frame, if that's your preference, or quilt in a hoop.

Following the quilting design, quilt with tiny, regular running stitches using a single strand of quilting thread in a short needle called a *between*. The needle action of hand quilting is rhythmic and repetitive: with one hand on top of the quilt, push the needle straight down through all layers; with the help of a finger pushing up from underneath, bring the needle back to the surface, taking a stitch in back that is the same length as the stitch in front (see Figure 5). Experienced hand quilters rock the needle with coordinated hand and finger movements, taking several stitches on the needle before drawing out the thread. Make a small knot in the end of the thread and pop it through the top fabric to lodge in the batting before bringing the needle out to start a seam. To finish, hide a backstitch or two under previous stitches, insert the needle into the batting, bring it out a distance away, and cut the thread where it emerges.

Many of the small projects in this book are designed for **machine quilting**. Instead of basting, safety-pin the layers together at close intervals, particularly beside the lines to be quilted. Adjust your machine for

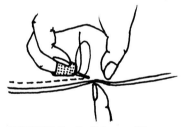

FIGURE 5. Quilting with one hand manipulating the needle on the surface and a finger of the other hand pushing up from below.

large stitches and balance the tension to accommodate thickness. Stitch slowly, gently stretching and holding the fabric being seamed to prevent the top layer from creeping ahead of the layers underneath. When machine-quilting seams start and stop within fabric rather than at the edge, pull the top thread to the back, tie to the bobbin thread, and bury the ends before cutting (see Edge Stitching, page 14). Although a fine transparent nylon thread especially for machine quilting is available, I quilted all projects with regular sewing thread that blended into the fabrics being stitched.

Whether quilting by hand or machine, to *quilt in the ditch* means to follow a pieced seam with seam allowances previously pressed closed by stitching off to the side without the seam allowances (because extra layers of fabric impede the needle), or to quilt right next to the edge of an appliqué.

FIGURE 6. Satin stitching.

SATIN STITCHING

Satin stitching covers a small area or thickens a line with threads laid smoothly alongside each other, concealing the fabric underneath. Figure 6 illustrates the hand stitch. To satin-stitch by machine, choose the zigzag width that's appropriate for the purpose and set the stitch length at 0. Appliqués can be applied with over-edge satin stitching by machine.

STUFFING

Stuffing makes a flat casing of fabric suitably three-dimensional. After stuffing, the casing should be taut and smooth, without lumps and unfilled areas, looking as if the stuffing had been poured inside rather than inserted piece by piece. To achieve this goal, use a long, blunt tool like a chopstick to work stuffing into areas that fingers can't reach; insert pieces of stuffing as large as the area you're filling can take; with controlled force, press stuffing against the casing and other stuffing and blend new stuffing into previous stuffing; check for even density and empty spaces by feeling with one hand while the other hand is doing the work; and monitor the developing shape by looking at stuffing-in-progress from arm's length.

The Four Seasonal Panels

Each section that follows is introduced by a pictorial panel: Spring on page 24, Summer on page 56, Fall on page 88, and Winter on page 116. In each panel, a silhouetted cat looks through a window at tree branches that reflect the season. The body of the cat and the branches are identical and in the same place in each panel; the head and tail positions of the cat and the condition of the branches (flowers, leaves, fruit, snow) change.

The panels are appliquéd by hand. The branches, flowers, leaves, and fruit require delicate needlework, but once you get used to manipulating shapes not much bigger than the size of your fingers, the appliqué is like any other, only daintier.

Each panel is 25" × 15½" when finished.

MATERIALS (for each panel)

100% cotton fabric:

14½" × 11½" of a sky-colored solid appropriate to the season for the background

5" × 10" of black for the branches

7" × 11" of a print for the cat

for Spring: a small piece of white for the flowers

for Summer: small pieces of bright green for the leaves and yellow-green for the green apples

for Fall: small pieces of darker green for the leaves and red for the apples

for Winter: 6" × 12" of white for the snow

22" × 18" of a print for the borders

28½" × 14½" of white for the lining

Other supplies:

for Spring: light green and pink embroidery floss

sewing thread that blends with the fabrics being stitched

2 dowels, each 18" long, ½" in diameter

DIRECTIONS

1. Enlarge one or all of the diagrams on pages 20–23. From the enlargement(s), make templates for the branches, cat, and Winter's snow; make templates for the other appliqués from the full-size patterns that accompany these instructions.

2. Trace and cut appliqués for the background from the appropriate fabrics (refer to the special instructions for Winter in step 3). Add ⅛"

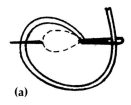

(a)

(b)

(c)

FIGURE 1. Making a bud (Spring) with a detached chain stitch.

seam allowances to the branches, tapering to $\frac{1}{16}''$ at the tip, and $\frac{1}{16}''$ seam allowances around all flower, leaf, and apple appliqués. Lightly trace the outlines of the branches, including Winter's snow, onto the background. The other appliqués may be visually positioned rather than traced.

3. Matching outlines, baste the branches into position before stitching. Appliqué the offshoot branches before the main branch. (**HINT:** Satin-stitch over the tip of each branch for $\frac{1}{8}''$ or so to capture straying threads.) Specifically, for each panel:

> After appliquéing Spring's branches, appliqué the seven flowers, pinning each one in position. Using two strands of pink embroidery floss, make single stitches that radiate out from the center of each flower as the pattern indicates. Using all six strands of green embroidery floss, embroider the buds using a detached chain stitch (see Figure 1), burying starts and stops behind the branch. (**HINT:** Use a small embroidery hoop to hold the fabric taut.)

> After appliquéing Summer's branches, appliqué twenty-seven leaves and five round green apples, pinning each one in position.

> After appliquéing Fall's branches, appliqué thirteen leaves and five apples, pinning each one in position.

> For each of Winter's branches, cut lengths of black and white bias as long as a branch and $\frac{3}{4}''$ wide. With a $\frac{1}{4}''$ seam allowance, sew the long sides of each pair of black and white strips together; trim the seam allowances $\frac{1}{16}''$ from the seam and press closed over the black. Baste the seam on each black-white strip to the snowline of the branch on the background and press to flatten. Matching snowline to seam, trace the outline of the snow-laden branch onto the strip; cut out $\frac{1}{8}''$ to $\frac{1}{16}''$ outside the outline and appliqué. Adding a $\frac{1}{4}''$ seam allowance, trace and cut snow to appliqué across the bottom of the background.

NOTE: *Dimensions include a $\frac{1}{4}''$ seam allowance.* Sew with right sides facing and edges matching.

---

4. From the border fabric, cut the following:

Border	Quantity	Size
Side	2	$3\frac{1}{2}'' \times 14\frac{1}{2}''$
Top	1	$5\frac{1}{2}'' \times 17\frac{1}{2}''$
Bottom	1	$9\frac{1}{2}'' \times 17\frac{1}{2}''$

5. Sew the side borders to opposite sides of the appliquéd background; sew the top and bottom borders across the background and side borders. Press the seam allowances closed over the borders. (Size after bordering: 28½″ × 17½″.)

6. For the cat, trace and cut body and head appliqués, adding seam allowances. Trace the cat's outline onto the panel. Matching outlines, appliqué the head first, then the body.

7. Fold 1″ at the sides of the panel to the back and press. Sew the 28½″ sides of the lining to the turned-back sides of the panel. Refolding on the pressed creases to center the lining, sew across the top and bottom, leaving a 4″ opening in the center of one of the seams. Turn right side out and press, folding the opening's seam allowances inside. On the back of the panel, draw lines 2½″ from the top and bottom. Turn the top and bottom edges to these lines and edgestitch through all layers, making channels for the dowels (see Figure 2). Slip dowels through the channels and hang the panel.

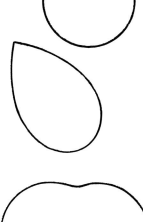

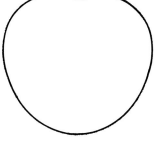

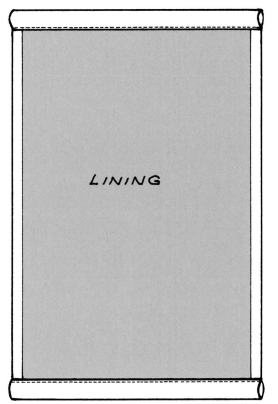

FIGURE 2. The back of a finished panel.

Full-size patterns for the flowers (Spring), green apples (Summer), leaves (Summer and Fall), and apples (Fall).

19

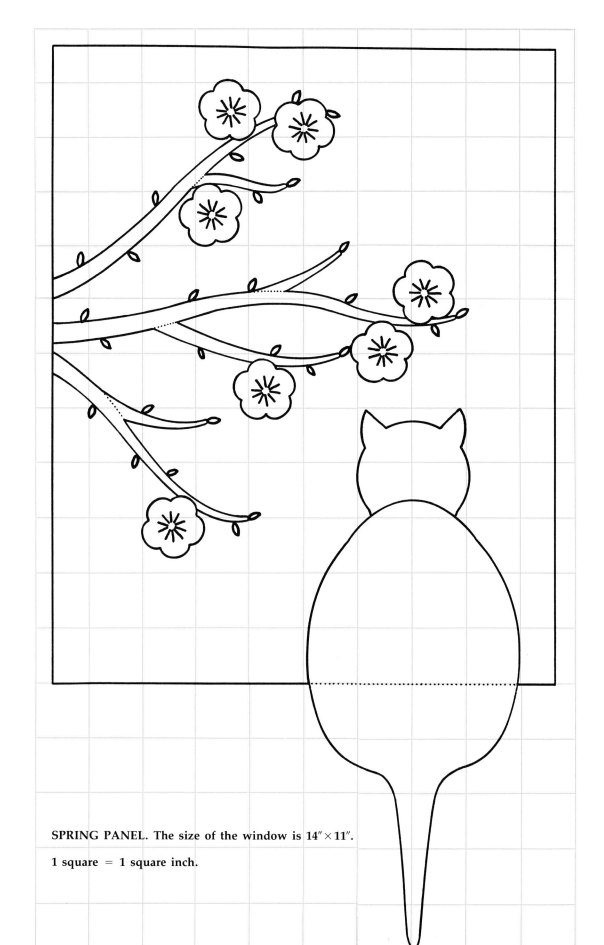

SPRING PANEL. The size of the window is 14″×11″.

1 square = 1 square inch.

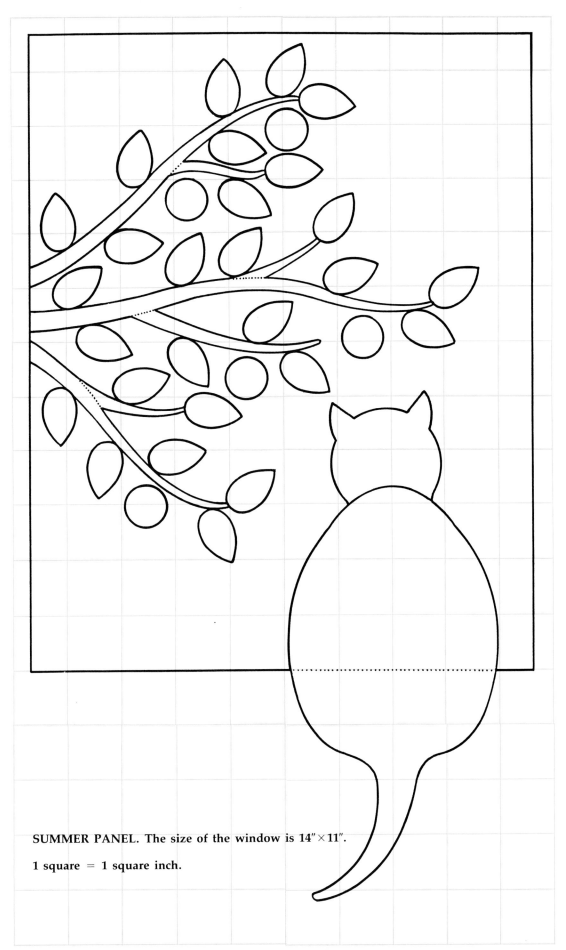

SUMMER PANEL. The size of the window is 14″ × 11″.

1 square = 1 square inch.

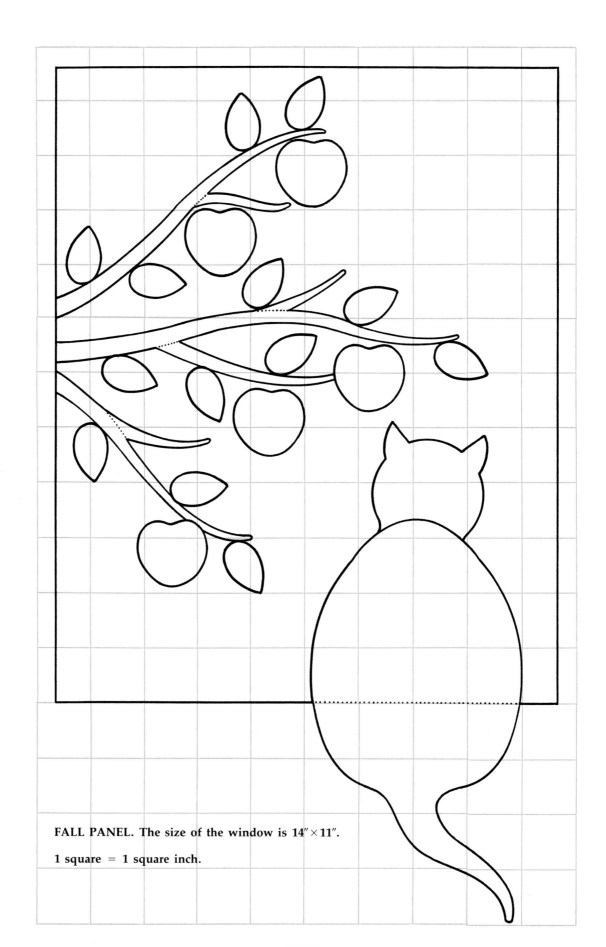

FALL PANEL. The size of the window is 14″×11″.

1 square = 1 square inch.

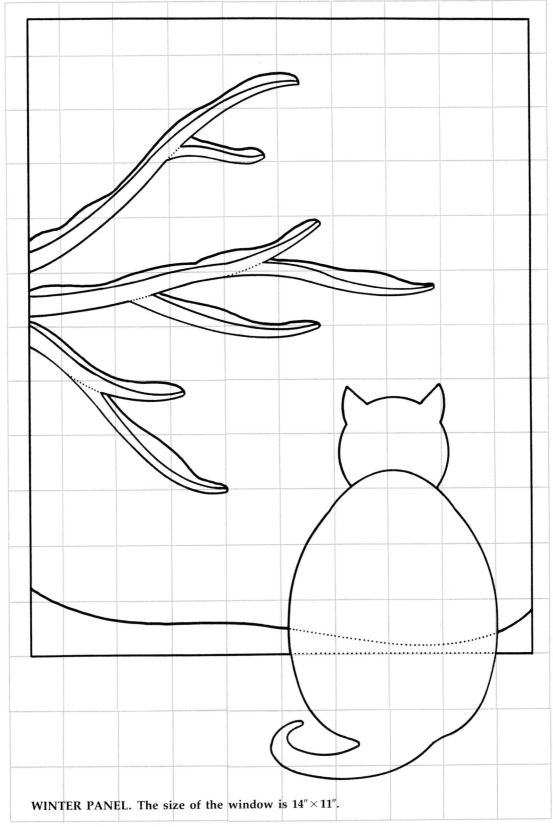

WINTER PANEL. The size of the window is 14″ × 11″.

1 square = 1 square inch.

Spring

Emerging from the white of winter, spring tints the landscape with tiny shoots of green and patches of pastels. With its buds and seedlings, blossoming trees, cleansing breezes, and nourishing rain, spring brings messages of hope and renewal.

Spring is the season to celebrate beginnings—marriages, births—and even, as you'll discover in the pages that follow, a new little tooth.

Instructions for the *Spring* panel start on page 17.

The Ultimate Gift for the Bride

To the American quiltmakers of generations past, the Bride's Quilt was both a sentimental favorite and a challenge. With hearts and doves as elements in its design, it symbolized marital bliss and expressed the hopes of the bride, her family, and friends whose fine needlework and creative talents it displayed. It was the showpiece of a bride's dower chest, the quilt she cherished and protected above all others.

Bridal Quilt

Like its historical antecedents, hearts and doves are featured in the design of "Tying the Knot"—as is another symbol from which this bride's quilt derives its name. Its message of love is conveyed by images in cloth and, like all those bride's quilts before, by every stitch of the appliquéing and quilting that goes into its construction.

"Tying the Knot," which measures 87″ × 75″, is composed of five panels, each one easily planned as work proceeds. I used a total of nineteen pastel prints and plains for the appliqués: thirteen yellow, peach, rose, and lavender coordinates for the flowers; three greens for the leaves; two blues for the doves; and a third blue print for the trellis bars that pattern the heart in the center. For your appliqués, you might include pieces of fabric that have meaning to the bride, adding memories to the significance of your "Tying the Knot" bridal quilt.

MATERIALS

100% cotton fabrics:

- 1½ yards of white, 45″ wide, for the central heart
- 5 yards of a pale background print, 45″ wide, for the area surrounding the central heart
- small pieces of assorted prints and solids for the flowers
- small pieces of green prints and solids for the leaves

8″ × 16″ of blue for the dove and 8″ × 12″ of a blue print for the doves' wings

5½ yards of a print or solid, 45″ wide, for the lining

1½ yards of a solid, 45″ wide, for the binding

*100% cotton bias tape, ½″ wide:**

12 yards of a blue print for the trellis bars

6½ yards of green for the vines

2 yards of pink or rose for the ribbon

¾ yard of a pink or rose print for the reverse side of the ribbon

*To make your own ½″ bias tape, cut and piece bias strips 1″ wide, turn a ¼″ seam allowance on both long sides to the back and press. Using a Clover tapemaker simplifies the procedure.

Other materials:

40″ × 40″ brown wrapping paper

a strip of cardboard 4″ wide, 30″ long (or longer)

steel-gray embroidery floss for the doves' eyes and beaks

thin quilt batting

sewing and quilting thread to match the fabrics being stitched

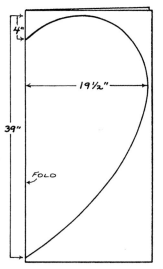

FIGURE 1. Measurements for cutting the heart pattern.

DIRECTIONS

Refer to the quilt diagram on page 31 when reading the following instructions. Although the design of "Tying the Knot" allows room for improvisation, it is your guide to the relationship and placement of the parts.

1. Make templates of the patterns on pages 32–34. Enlarge and complete the quilting diagrams on page 28.

2. Fold a piece of 40″ × 40″ brown wrapping paper in half. Applying the measurements specified in Figure 1, outline and cut out a heart. Referring to Figure 2, outline the trellis pattern that crisscrosses the

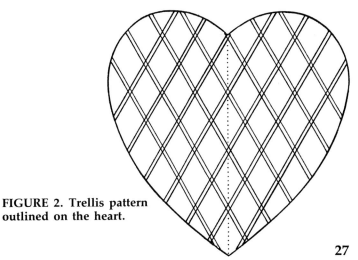

FIGURE 2. Trellis pattern outlined on the heart.

27

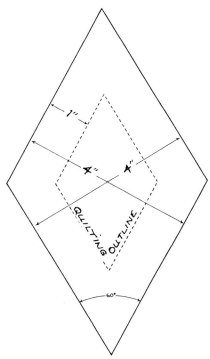

FIGURE 3. The diamond shape that is surrounded by ½″ bars to create the trellis pattern.

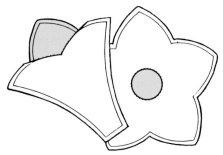

FIGURE 4. Floral appliqués, centers attached, ready to stitch in place.

heart with bold, black lines. Locate the tip of a diamond (see Figure 3) at the cleft of the heart and proceed from there, using a cardboard strip 4″ wide to draw lines separated by bars ½″ wide.

3. Cut a heart from white fabric (don't add a seam allowance). Pin the fabric heart over the paper heart and trace the trellis pattern onto the fabric. Appliqué strips of ½″ bias tape over the trellis bars.

Note: Panel dimensions include a ½″ seam allowance. Assemble with right sides facing and edges matching.

---

4. From the background print, cut a center panel 51″ × 45″. Baste the heart to the center of the panel with zigzag machine stitching. Cut away the background fabric that lies under the heart.

5. Surround the heart with a border of appliquéd flowers and leaves. Start at the top of the heart. Cutting flowers and leaves as needed, establish small groupings of flowers and leaves, stitch them down, cut and arrange further groupings, stitch, and so on until the edge of the heart is entirely hidden behind appliqués. Appliqué centers to the flowers before stitching in place (see Figure 4). Note that the base of flower 2 must be tucked under flower 1 or covered with leaves; that the base of each leaf must be concealed under another leaf or a flower; and that what's underneath is appliquéd first, what's on top is appliquéd last. At the sides of the heart, finish stitching any leaves or flowers that extend into the seam allowances after the side panels have been seamed to the center panel.

6. Cut out and appliqué a pair of doves over the nest of flowers and leaves prepared at the base of the heart. Stitch bodies first, then wings.

7. Cut two side panels 51″ × 16″ from the background print. Press a guideline crease down the center of each panel. At the base of each panel, attach two 40″ lengths of green bias tape at the crease. Curve the tapes up beside the crease, weaving them gracefully across each other in two places. (If you prefer, you can draw tape lines first, tracing curves from the side of the paper heart pattern.) Trimming and tapering the ends of these tapes to points, appliqué the vines. Appliqué two flowers with leaves onto the vines, but ignore the cluster at the base of the vines until later. (**Hint:** Appliqué the vines to one panel; press face down over the second panel; use the imprint left by the pressing as guidelines for the vines on the second panel.)

8. Machine-stitch the side panels to the center panel. Press the seam allowances open.

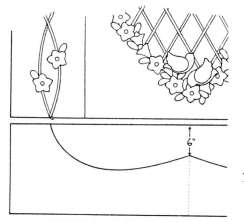

FIGURE 5. Guideline marked on the bottom panel.

FIGURE 6. Center knot with reversed sections replaced with a different bias tape.

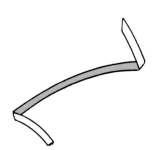

FIGURE 7. One end of the ribbon with reversed section replaced.

9. Cut top and bottom panels, each 19″ × 75″, from the background print. For the bottom panel, draw a vine guideline that curves down from the vines on the side panels and up in the center, as indicated in Figure 5. Use the side of the heart pattern to define the curve. Starting in the center of the panel, appliqué flower-and-leaf clusters, connected with pieces of green bias tape, over the guideline. With right sides together, machine-stitch the bottom panel to the center-and-side panels (press the seam allowance open) before appliquéing the floral clusters that straddle the seamline.

10. Pin-baste two A doves (reverse the pattern for one of the doves) to the top panel. For the knot, draw a circular guideline 6″ across in the center toward the bottom of the panel. (HINT: Trace around a salad plate.) Using the side of the heart pattern to define a curve, draw guidelines connecting the beaks of the doves to the central circle. Appliqué solid bias tape ribbon over these guidelines, weaving the ribbon over and under for the knot and folding the ribbon wrong side up at the sides of the circle (see Figure 6). Replace the reversed ribbon with patterned bias tape. Draw guidelines and appliqué the ends of the ribbon (see Figure 7), again replacing the reversed section with patterned bias tape. Appliqué the doves.

11. Machine-stitch the top panel across the quilt top and press the seam allowance open. Embroider the eyes and beak of each dove with satin stitching. Press the quilt top. Press light guideline creases that extend the lines of the central trellis pattern out to the edge of the quilt in several places.

12. Referring to the diagram on page 31, mark the top for quilting. First, trace the wreath of flowers around the knot and trace the two hearts at the lower sides of the center heart. Then, using the guideline creases as touch points, mark the background trellis bars to the top's outside edges, tracing from the paper heart pattern and using the cardboard strip. Mark the small diamonds inside the trellis diamonds using a special template (see Figure 3).

13. Seam two 2¾-yard lengths of lining fabric together; press the seam allowances open. Trim the lining and batting to 92″ × 80″, 2½″ larger all around than the quilt top. Smooth the batting over the lining, right side down, and center the quilt top over both. Baste the layers together for quilting in a frame or hoop. Quilt from the center to the edges, quilting next to every appliquéd edge as well as quilting over the lines marked on the top. Don't forget to quilt the lines inside the birds' wings. Trim the batting and lining to the sides of the top.

14. Cut and piece 9 yards plus 6″ of binding, 2½″ wide, and prepare a doubled binding. With the appliquéd side of the quilt up, sew the

30

"Tying the Knot" bridal quilt. Finished size: 87″ × 75″.

1 square = 8 square inches.

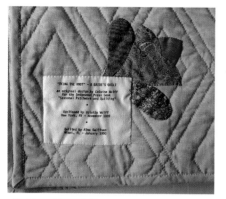

binding around the quilt ½″ from the matched cut edges, mitering the corners. Turning the binding over the quilt's edge to the back, blindstitch the binding to the lining.

15. To the back of your "Tying the Knot" quilt, attach a label with your name, the date and place, and any other information you want to record for posterity, such as shown in photo on left.

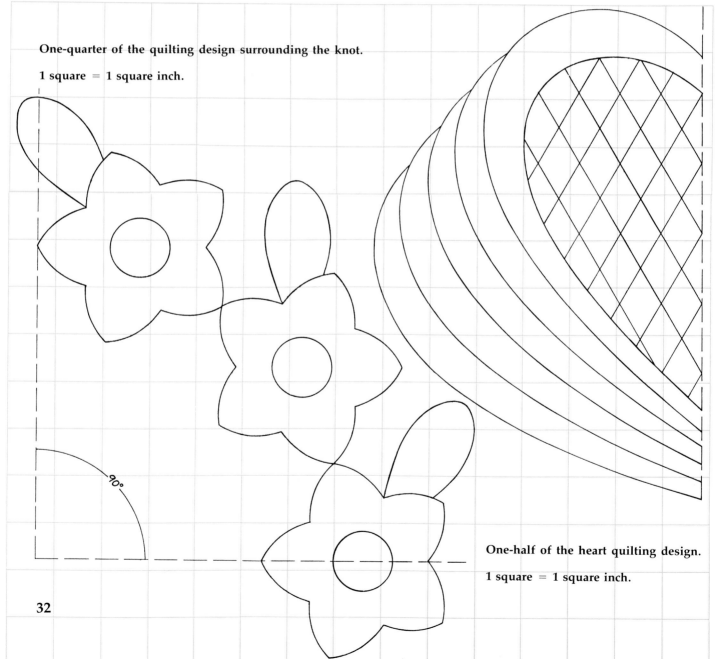

One-quarter of the quilting design surrounding the knot.

1 square = 1 square inch.

90°

One-half of the heart quilting design.

1 square = 1 square inch.

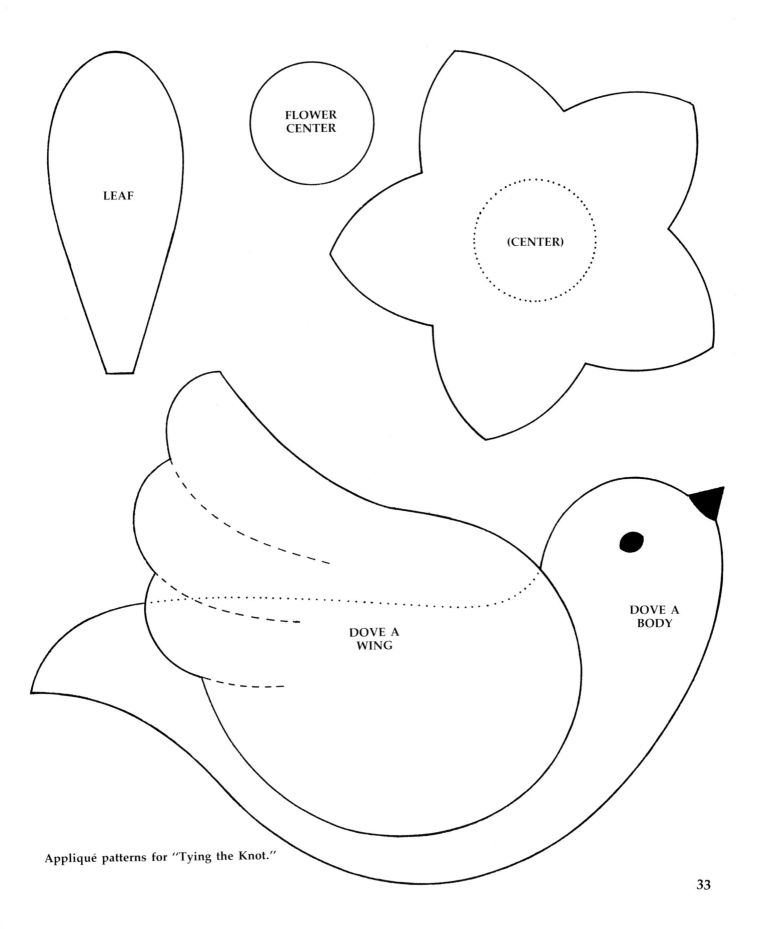

LEAF

FLOWER CENTER

(CENTER)

DOVE A WING

DOVE A BODY

Appliqué patterns for "Tying the Knot."

33

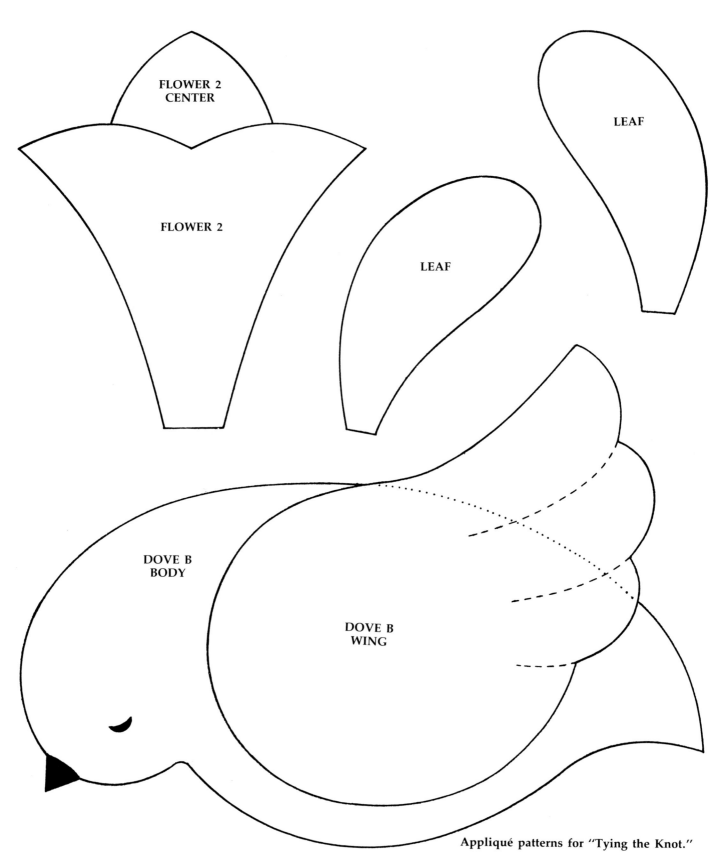

FLOWER 2
CENTER

FLOWER 2

LEAF

LEAF

DOVE B
BODY

DOVE B
WING

Appliqué patterns for "Tying the Knot."

34

Bridal Fancies

Satin and pearls on a log cabin base . . . the elegant wedding and humble beginnings . . . the kind of contrast that captivates a quilter's fancy with its implications.

Ring Pillow

For this 8″ × 8″ satin pillow, the central square of the log cabin pattern, the cabin's floor, is surrounded with a lacy ruffle to contain the wedding rings. The logs that surround the central square, the walls of the cabin, are studded with pearls.

Embroider the initials of the bridal couple and their wedding date on a corner of the pillow. Enclose the ring pillow in an acid-free box wrapped in acid-free tissue paper so that the bride can preserve it in mint condition for her daughter to use when she gets married.

MATERIALS

¼ yard of white bridal satin
an 8½″ square of white muslin
30″ of white lace, ¾″ wide
polyester stuffing
white sewing thread
pearl beads
12″ of white satin ribbon, ⅛″ wide

DIRECTIONS

NOTE: Dimensions include a ¼″ seam allowance. Sew with right sides facing, edges matching, unless directed otherwise.

1. Make a working copy of the center square pattern on page 36.

2. From the satin, measure and cut an 8½″ square for the pillow lining; trace and cut a center square. Use the remaining satin to cut strips 1½″ wide as needed for the log cabin patchwork.

3. Folding the 8½″ square of muslin diagonally from corner to corner, press guideline creases that cross in the center. Matching corners to creases, machine-baste the satin center square to the muslin. Gather

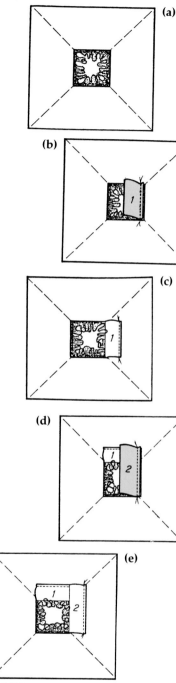

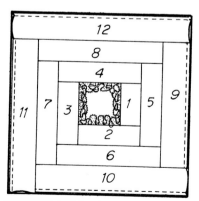

30″ of lace to 10″, distributing the gathers evenly. Matching edges, baste the lace around the center square. Overlap the ends of the lace and hand-stitch together (see Figure 1a).

4. Construct the log cabin block:

Matching the top and right edges, sew a 1½″ strip to the center square over the lace. Cut the strip even with the lower edge of the square (see Figure 1b). Open the strip; machine-baste its right edge to the muslin (see Figure 1c).

Matching the top and right edges, sew a 1½″ strip to the cut edge of the previously applied strip and the central square over the lace. Cut the strip even with the lower edge of the square (see Figure 1d). Open the strip; machine-baste its right edge to the muslin (see Figure 1e).

Continue as above, adding new strips to the logs already in place, until your log cabin block looks like Figure 2. Your final row of logs may not quite reach the edge of the 8½″ muslin foundation, but it must be square even if smaller. Trim the muslin to the edge of the strips.

5. Sew the lining, trimmed to size, to the log cabin top, leaving a 3″ opening in the center of one side. After trimming the corners diagonally, turn right side out.

6. Stuff until the pillow is plump and pleasingly firm. Ladder-stitch the opening closed.

7. Decorate with pearls scattered around the central square. Tack the center of 12″ of satin ribbon to the middle of the central square; thread a ribbon through each ring and tie in a bow to hold.

FIGURE 1. (a) Center square and gathered lace basted to an 8½″ foundation square; (b) the first log stitched, trimmed, (c) opened and basted to the foundation; (d) the second log stitched, trimmed, (e) opened and basted.

FIGURE 2. The finished log cabin square, numbered in the sequence of log application.

LOG CABIN
CENTER SQUARE

Bride's Purse

The first time I saw a bride carry a bag at her wedding reception, I thought it was strange—until I noticed the envelopes that passed from the guests into her hands and understood that she was carrying the wedding bank. Since then I've seen many brides carry bags at receptions for just such a purpose, but I've never seen a bag that complemented the bride's gown and the occasion. Mostly, they were squares of bridal fabric with handles, strictly utilitarian. This one is functional, but it's also so pretty that it might even appeal to the bride who has made other collection arrangements.

Its design is a log cabin constructed on the diagonal. I decorated my example with a spray of fabric rosettes, a ribbon bow, and pearls. Your bride might prefer real flowers or appliqués of lace.

The example measures 5" in diameter and 9" high. If your bride requires a roomier interior, enlarge the circular base, measure half its circumference, and use that measurement as the width of a log cabin block. You'll also need to widen the drawstring top.

MATERIALS

⅓ yard of white bridal satin

10" × 17" of white muslin

10" × 23" of white lining fabric

two large eyelets

2 yards of white rattail

white ribbon rosettes, white ribbon, and pearl beads

a 5" square of stiff, sturdy cardboard

white sewing thread

DIRECTIONS

NOTE: Patterns and dimensions include a ¼" *seam allowance.* Sew with right sides facing, edges matching, unless directed otherwise.

---

1. Make a full-size copy of the base pattern on page 40 and a copy of the center square pattern used for the ring pillow, on page 36.

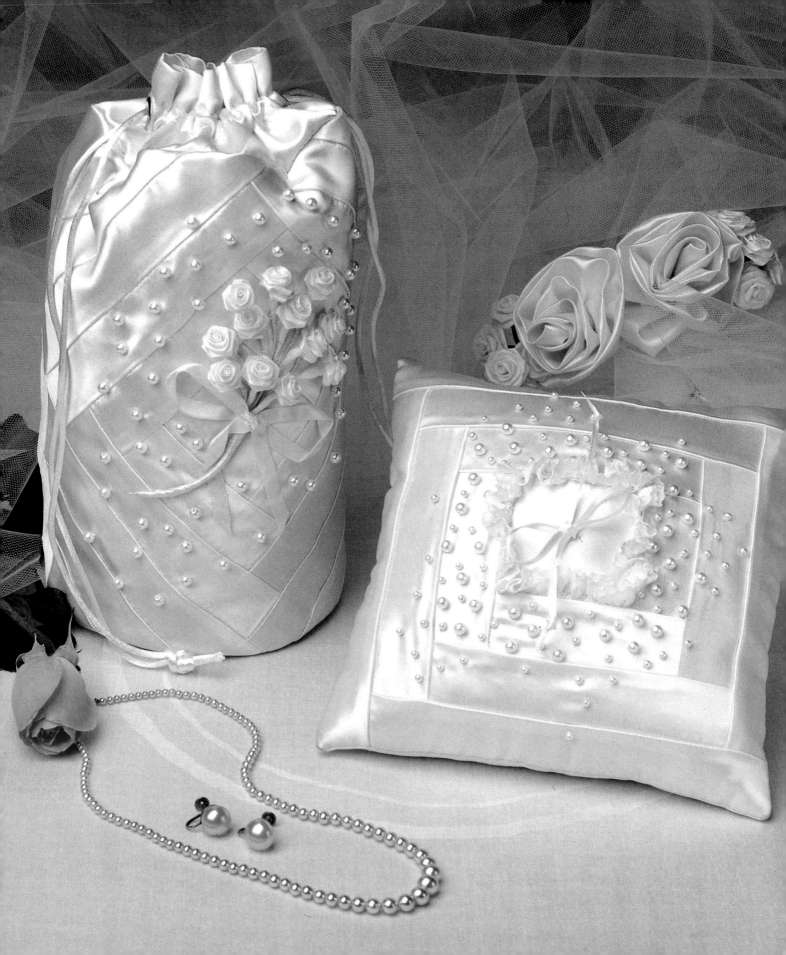

2. Cut the following:

Fabric	Pattern Piece	Quantity	Size
Satin*	center square	2	pattern
	base	1	pattern
	drawstring top	2	5″ × 8½″
Muslin	foundation	2	10″ × 8½″
Lining	side	1	10″ × 17″
	base	1	pattern

*Use the remaining satin to cut strips 1½″ wide as needed for the log cabin patchwork.

3. Folding each muslin foundation in half from side to side, press two guideline creases that cross in the center. Matching corners to creases, machine-baste a center square to the center of each foundation.

4. Proceeding as described for the ring pillow (page 36, step 4), construct diagonal log cabin patchwork around the central square. Use 1½″ strips for the logs. When the foundation is covered with logs (see Figure 1), trim the logs that extend over its edges. Press, lining side up, on a padded surface.

5. Matching the log seams, sew the 10″ sides of the rectangles together, making a cylinder. Press the seam allowances open.

6. Sew the 5″ sides of the drawstring top pieces together, making a cylinder, and press the seam allowances open. With the right side outside, fold in half and press. Unfold and, following the instructions on the package, attach a large eyelet 1″ down from the fold over each seam. With a zipper foot on your machine, stitch a drawstring channel as wide as the eyelets around the folded top as Figure 2 illustrates.

7. Sew the 10″ sides of the lining together and press the seam allowance open. Pin the drawstring top, eyelet side down, over the right side of the patchwork at the top, matching the side seams. Pin the lining, right side inside, over both. Sew all layers together around the top (see Figure 3). Turn right side out. Sewing on the seamline, machine-baste the lining to the patchwork around the bottom. Clip the seam allowance up to the basting every ½″.

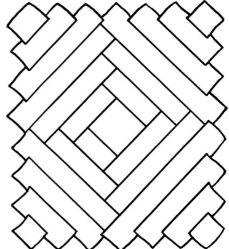

FIGURE 1. Diagonally constructed log cabin rectangle before trimming.

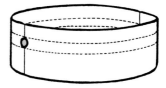

FIGURE 2. Drawstring top with stitched drawstring channel and eyelet openings at the side seams.

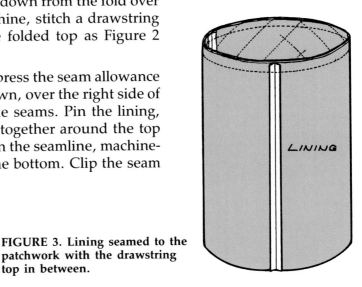

FIGURE 3. Lining seamed to the patchwork with the drawstring top in between.

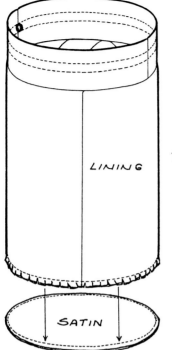

FIGURE 4. Preparing to seam the base to the purse.

8. Machine-baste the satin base to its lining. With the satin sides together, hand-baste, then machine-stitch the base to the patchwork cylinder (see Figure 4). Changing to a wide, closely spaced zigzag, stitch over the seam allowance. Turn the purse right side out.

9. Thread a 1-yard length of rattail into a large-eyed, blunt needle or bodkin. Work through the drawstring channel, going into and out of the same eyelet. Knot the ends of the cord together. Repeat with another yard of rattail through the other eyelet.

10. Fit a piece of stiff cardboard, cut slightly smaller than the seamline on the base pattern, inside the purse. Embellish the outside with rosettes, ribbon, and pearl beads.

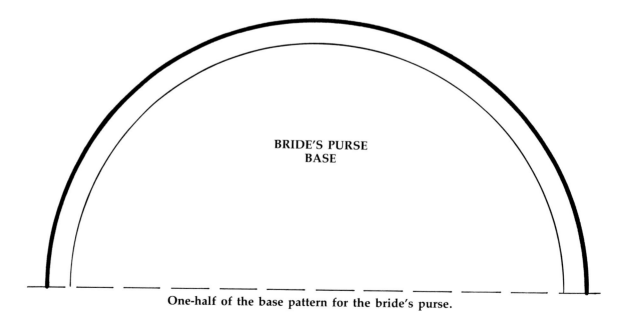

BRIDE'S PURSE
BASE

One-half of the base pattern for the bride's purse.

Suppose It's Twins

If it is, such an event should be commemorated with a very special gift, like a pair of quilts. Sunbonnet Sue and Overall Bill, who have been popular subjects for quilt designs since 1900, suit the occasion perfectly. Suppose it's two girls—two Sunbonnet Sue quilts with different colorings; for two boys, two Overall Bill quilts with color changes and different kites. And one or the other, whichever fits, would delight any mother who's just had a baby.

Two Sunbonnet Quilts

Sunbonnets have definite characteristics. The face of a typical Sunbonnet is forever hidden by a bonnet's brim and the Sunbonnet is always busy doing something. These interpretations, which I call "The Sunbonnet Twins on a Breezy Spring Day," follow the folklore. In her quilt, Sue loses a balloon. In his quilt, Bill flies a kite. Their stories unfold in four appliquéd pictures that utilize simple pattern manipulations to advance the action in succeeding blocks.

Each Sunbonnet quilt measures 39″ × 31″.

MATERIALS (for each quilt)

100% cotton fabrics in coordinating colors, 45″ wide, unless noted otherwise:

½ yard of white for the blocks

small pieces of appropriate prints and solids for the appliqués

⅓ yard of a print for the sashing

3″ × 27″ of a print for the corner squares

½ yard of a print for the border

1 yard of a print or solid for the lining

¾ yard of a solid for the binding

Other supplies:

45″ × 36″ of batting

sewing and quilting thread to match the fabrics being stitched

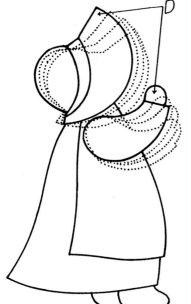

FIGURE 1. Varying bonnet and arm positions for Sunbonnet Sue.

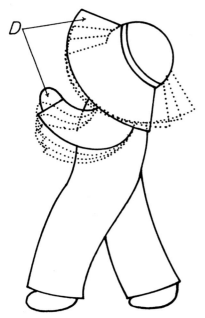

FIGURE 2. Changing hat and arm positions for Overall Bill.

DIRECTIONS

1. Make an appliqué template for each numbered part of the Sunbonnet Sue or Overall Bill figures on pages 48–49 and make a template of the full-size figure as well.

2. From white fabric, cut four rectangular foundation blocks, each 15″ × 11″ (½″ seam allowance included). Press two guideline creases into each block: the first, 2½″ from the bottom edge; the second, 2½″ from the left edge for Sue, 2½″ from the right edge for Bill.

3. Tracing around the templates, cut out the appliqués from the appropriate fabrics, adding seam allowances.

4. Appliqué block D first. Lightly trace the silhouette of the figure onto the foundation block, aligning the broken line (line D on Overall Bill) on the figure to the guideline creases. Match the outline of each appliqué to the corresponding outline traced on the block. Appliqué the figure from the feet up, in order as the parts are numbered. Before appliquéing to the foundation, appliqué the hand to the arm and the band to the bonnet. Place the balloons and kite as the diagrams on page 45 indicate and appliqué.

5. Appliqué block C next, then blocks B and A:

   For each Sunbonnet Sue block: Align the broken line on the figure to the guideline creases. Lightly trace the silhouette of the figure, omitting the arm and bonnet. Appliqué the shoes, dress, and apron. Place the current block over the previously finished block, matching the edges; trace new arm and bonnet positions using the appliqué templates, lowering both a little more for each block as Figure 1 indicates. Appliqué the arm-hand and the bonnet-with-band. Position and appliqué the balloons as illustrated. Note that the tip of Sue's bonnet overlaps one balloon in block B and both balloons in block A, therefore these balloons must be appliquéd before the bonnet.

   For each Overall Bill block: Align the appropriately lettered broken line on the figure to the guideline creases. Lightly trace the outline of the figure, omitting the arm and bonnet. Appliqué the shoes and overalls. Place the current block over the previously finished block, matching shoe and overall outlines; trace new arm and bonnet positions using the appliqué templates, lowering both a little more for each block as Figure 2 indicates. Appliqué the arm-hand and the bonnet-with-band. Position and appliqué the kite as illustrated.

44

NOTE: The following cutting dimensions include a ½″ *seam allowance*. Sew with right sides facing, edges matching, unless indicated otherwise.

6. Crosscut the 3″×27″ strip of fabric into nine 3″×3″ corner squares. From the sashing fabric, cut four strips 3″×45″. Crosscut these strips into six 15″ and six 11″ sashing strips. Sew the 11″ sashing strips to corner blocks and the 15″ sashing strips to the appliquéd blocks as illustrated in Figure 3. Sew these rows together, matching all seams that cross. Press the seam allowances closed over the sashing.

7. From the border fabric, cut two side borders, each 3″×35″, and a top and bottom border, each 3″×31″. Sew the side borders to the sashed blocks, then the top and bottom borders (see Figure 4). Press these seam allowances closed.

8. Following the diagrams on page 47, mark the quilting lines inside

FIGURE 3. Left: Seaming corner squares, sashing strips, and blocks together in rows.

FIGURE 4. Above: Adding a border around the assembled blocks.

each appliquéd block; draw balloon and kite strings freely and outline a quilted frame 2″ inside the edge of each block.

9. Smooth the batting over the lining, right side down, and center the quilt top over both (the lining and batting will be about 2½″ larger all around than the top). Baste the layers together for quilting in a frame or hoop. Quilt next to every appliquéd edge and quilt over the lines drawn on the blocks. Quilt in the ditch around the sashing, the corner blocks, and the border. (**HINT:** After quilting, you can emphasize the balloon and kite strings by whipping the quilting stitches. Thread a blunt tapestry needle with two strands of embroidery floss; without penetrating the fabric, run the needle under each stitch.) Trim the batting and lining to the edge of the top and baste the layers together around all sides, sewing within the seam allowance.

10. Cut and piece 4 yards plus 8″ of binding, 2½″ wide, and prepare a doubled binding. With the appliquéd side of the quilt up, sew the binding around the banner ½″ from the matched cut edges, mitering the corners. Turning the binding over the quilt's edge to the back, blindstitch the binding to the lining.

11. To the back of your Sunbonnet quilt, attach a label with your name, the date and place, the baby's name, and any other information you would like to record.

The four Sunbonnet Sue blocks.

1 square = 4 square inches.

The four Overall Bill blocks.

1 square = 4 square inches.

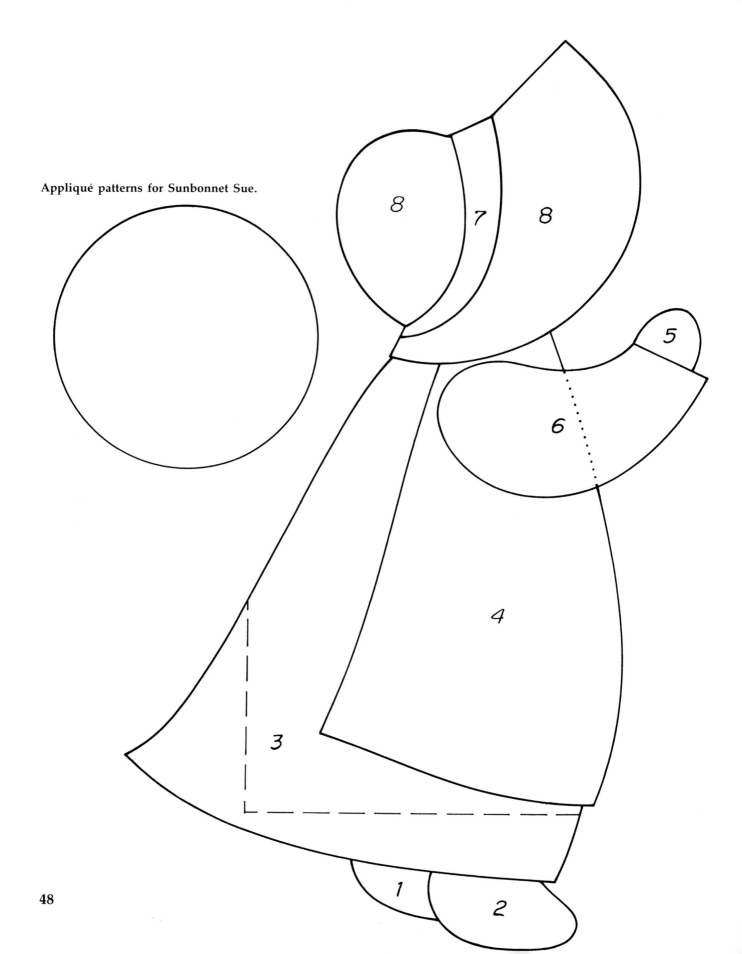

Appliqué patterns for Sunbonnet Sue.

48

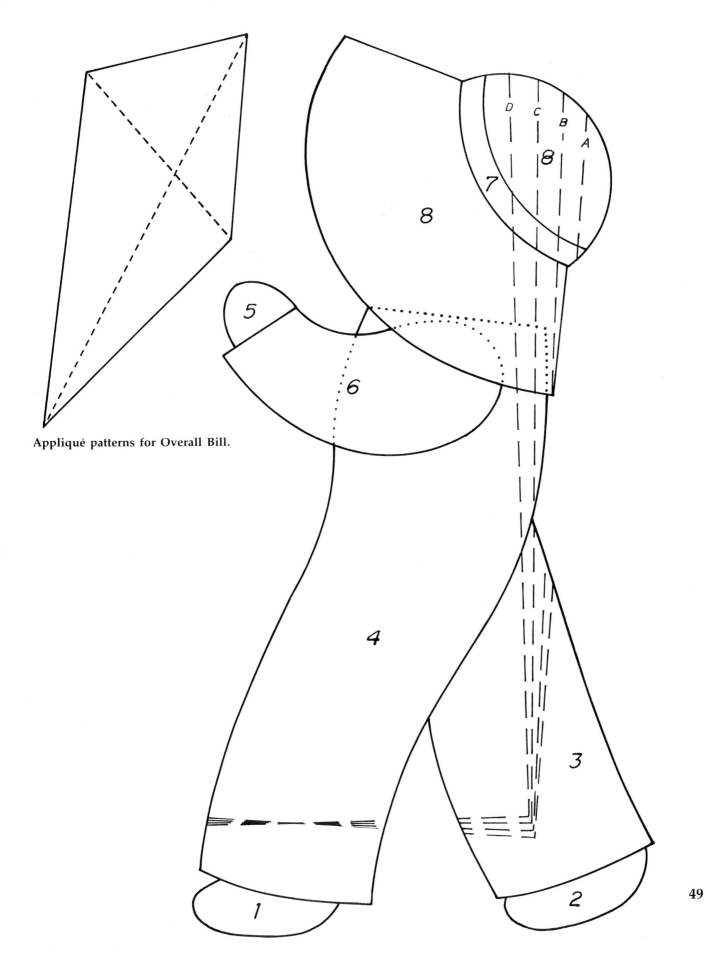

Appliqué patterns for Overall Bill.

8

5

6

7

D C B A

8

4

3

1

2

Tessie, the Tooth Fairy

Tessie has a mission. She wants children to grow strong, healthy teeth. To spread her message, she flies in to visit boys and girls when their secondary teeth are beginning to appear, and she makes a trade.

"A token for a tooth," she whispers as she settles on the bed beside a sleeping child. Very gently, she feels underneath the child's pillow, searching for the baby tooth she knows the child just lost that day.

The next morning the child wakes up to discover that the tooth has been exchanged for a coin—and there's Tessie, who presents a brand-new toothbrush with a note that says, "Be sure to brush!"

Pillow Doll

Made from cloth and stuffing, Tessie's called a pillow doll because, although her silhouette is shapely when she's viewed from the front, she's really just a contoured pillow. She measures 10½" from toe tip to top of head and her arms move up and down.

MATERIALS

100% cotton fabrics:
 5" × 6" of unbleached muslin for the face and hands
 9" × 20" of a print for the body
 a 3" square of a coordinating solid for the feet
 4" × 5" of a coordinating print or solid for the pockets
 two coordinating cotton solids, each 5" × 9", for the bow wig

Other supplies:
 11" × 14" of nylon net for the wings
 polyester stuffing
 blue, brown, rose, and white sewing thread as well as thread that blends with the fabrics being stitched
 18" of satin ribbon, ⅛" wide
 a child's toothbrush with a small card attached

FIGURE 1. Machine-embroidered facial features.

DIRECTIONS

NOTE: Patterns (except the foot and wing patterns) and dimensions include a ¼" *seam allowance*. Sew with right sides facing, edges matching, unless directed otherwise.

1. Make working copies of the patterns on pages 54 and 55.

2. Cut a 4" square of unbleached muslin. Trace one outline of the head pattern and the facial features onto the muslin's right side. Pin the muslin, right side up, over a square of white paper. Working slowly, machine-embroider the features as in Figure 1:

   With tiny stitches, define the eyebrow/nose line with a seam of brown thread.

   Changing to blue thread, a wide zigzag, and 0 stitch length setting, fill in the eyes with radiating stitches. Start with the needle in the center dot, stitch out and in, pivot a fraction on the needle, stitch out and in, pivot again, and so on until the circle is complete.

   Changing to rose thread and the smallest zigzag with a satin-stitch setting, define the mouth. Gently remove the paper and cut out the head.

3. From appropriate fabrics, cut two body pieces, one for the front and one reversed for the back; cut a front pocket 2¼" square and a back pocket 4" × 1½". Turn the seam allowances on all sides of each pocket to the back and press. Zigzag over the edge of the seam allowance at the top of each pocket (a short side of the back pocket). Edgestitch the pockets to the body front and back where the pattern indicates (see Figure 2).

4. Trace the outlines of the foot patterns onto the wrong side of fabric 3" square, folded in half. Stitch over the outlines, leaving the straight edges unseamed. Cut out ⅛" from the seams, ¼" from the straight edges. Turn right side out and stuff lightly. Matching letters as the patterns indicate, baste the feet to the body front (see Figure 2).

5. Cut a head back from the body fabric. Stitching from ● to ●, sew the embroidered muslin head to the body front and the head back to the body back. Stitch over the seamline between the ○'s. Seam the front to the back, leaving an opening between the ○'s. Clip the seam allowance at the inside body curve, trim diagonally at the corner, and turn the casing right side out.

6. Stuff until the fabric is stretched smooth and wrinkle-free over the filling condensed inside. Folding the seam allowances on the machine stitching to the inside, ladder-stitch the opening closed.

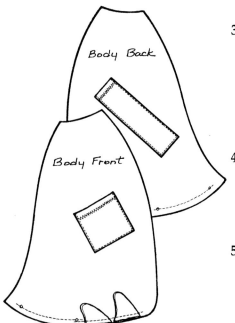

FIGURE 2. Body front and back with pockets attached, openings stay-stitched, and feet basted to the front.

Body Back

Body Front

7. Cut four hands from the muslin and four arms, two reversed, from the body fabric. Sew the hands to the arms and then stitch the hand-arm pairs together, leaving an opening between the ○'s. Clip the seam allowances at the inside curves, trim to ⅛″ around the hands, and turn right side out. Stuff and ladder-stitch the openings closed.

8. Stab-pin the arms to the body at the X positions marked on the patterns. With a long, double-threaded needle, sew the arms to the body as if you were attaching buttons. Run the needle through the body and out one arm; back into that arm, through the body, and out the other arm; run the needle back and forth twice again, always pulling the thread taut to hold the arms firmly against the body. Secure the thread under one arm (see Figure 3).

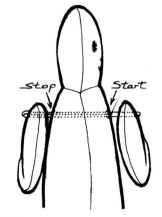

FIGURE 3. The path of the thread that attaches the movable arms to the body.

9. From each of the solids selected for the bow wig, cut six strips of bias 3″ long, 1″ wide. Tie a knot in the center of each strip. After trimming the ends evenly, tack to the seamline around the head, framing the face attractively.

10. With a black pen, trace the outline of the wings onto white paper. Cut the nylon net into four pieces 5½″ × 7″; stack and pin the pieces to the paper over the outline. Straight-stitch over the outline, then change to a medium-width zigzag and satin-stitch over the straight stitching (see Figure 4). Remove the paper. Fold the wings together and press. Placing the top of the fold 1″ down from the neck seam, sew the wings to the body, backstitching over the fold into the back seam. Tack the wings together at the top for ¼″.

11. Tack the center of the ribbon to the body just above the wings and knot the ends together. Put the toothbrush into the back pocket and Tessie's ready to fly.

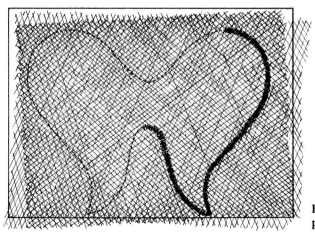

FIGURE 4. Nylon net wings partially satin-stitched to paper.

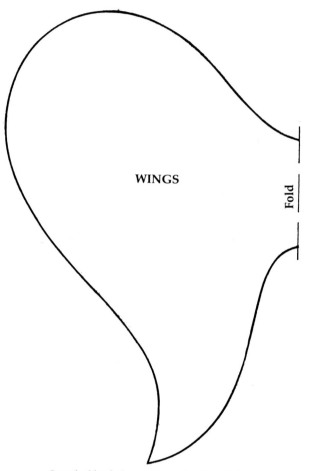

WINGS

Fold

One-half of the pattern for Tessie's wings.

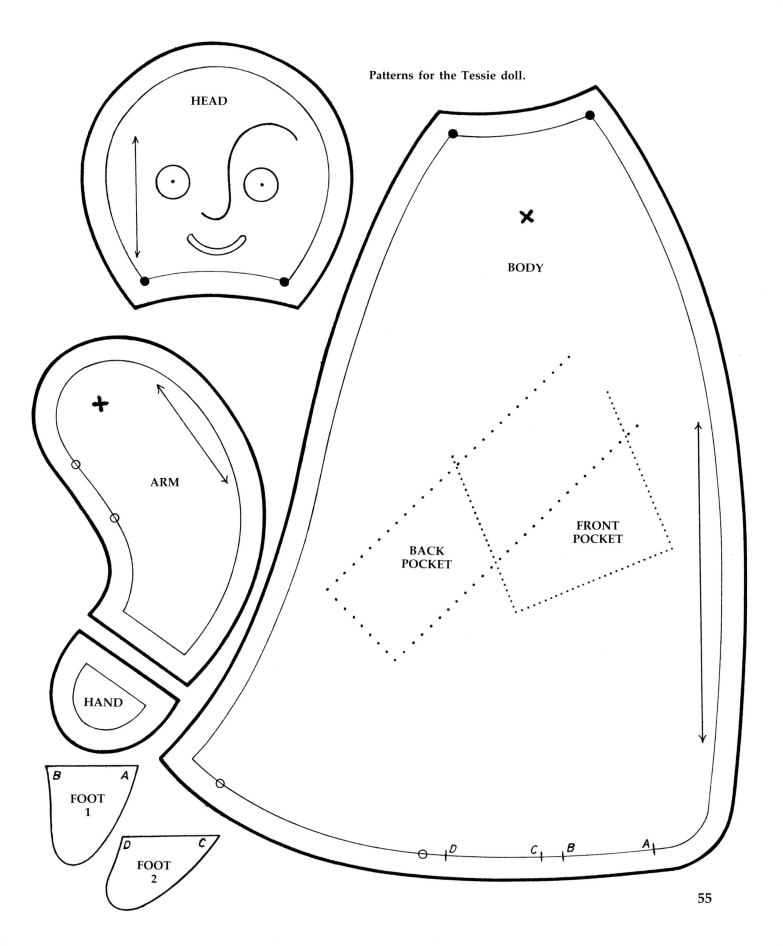

Patterns for the Tessie doll.

HEAD

BODY

ARM

FRONT POCKET

BACK POCKET

HAND

B   A
FOOT 1

D   C
FOOT 2

D   C   B   A

55

Summer

Summer intensifies the colors that spring began. It flaunts the spectrum with hues that are vivid, clear, and contrasting.

Summer's long sunny days, blue skies, fleecy clouds, lush green foliage, flowers, and heat turn everyone's focus out-of-doors. It's a time for picnics, barbecues, languid siestas, and little girls running barefoot through the grass.

Instructions for the *Summer* panel start on page 17.

Hooray for the Red, White, and Blue

Traditionally, Americans celebrate the 4th of July with food and fireworks. While the fireworks shouldn't be your responsibility, you could be producing a picnic or barbecue that will capture the spirit of the day with this patriotic ensemble.

Bandanna Mats

Unexpectedly, bandannas make rather elegant roll-up-and-tie picnic mats. Tucked into one of the patch pockets stitched to a mat, a second bandanna becomes a ready-made napkin and, with a red, white, and blue color scheme, the combination is 4th of July with a touch of the Old West.

Since bandannas differ somewhat in size and pattern, the picnic mats they make will also vary, so adapt the directions that follow accordingly. Before converting your bandannas into mats, be sure to preshrink.

MATERIALS (for one bandanna mat)

two bandannas, 100% cotton, approximately 21" square, one for the mat and the other for the napkin

scraps of contrasting checked, polka-dot, or striped cotton for the pockets

6"×8" of muslin lining for the pockets

21"×21" of a contrasting checked, polka-dot, or striped cotton for the lining

sewing thread to match the fabrics being stitched

DIRECTIONS

NOTE: Sew with right sides facing, edges matching, and a ¼" seam allowance.

1. Cut two pockets, each 3¾" × 5½", with linings to match. Sew each pocket to a lining around the outside, leaving a 2" opening centered in one short side. After trimming the corner seam allowances diagonally, turn right side out and press. With openings at the bottom, pin the pockets to opposite corners of the bandanna, relating their placement to the bandanna's design and the diameter of a plate. Edgestitch each pocket to the bandanna. Divide the pocket on the right into three equal sections with two internal seams as Figure 1 illustrates.

2. Trim the bandanna ½" or less from the printed border (when finished, the printed labeling in the border should be hidden). Make a tube tie from one length of the trim (fold lengthwise, seam the edges together, and turn right side out with a tube-turning device). Fold the tie in half and pin the fold to the seam allowance at the left corner of the bandanna. With the tie in between, seam the bandanna to the lining, sewing outside the printed border of the bandanna. Leave a 3" opening in one side. After trimming the corner seam allowances diagonally, turn right side out, press, and ladder-stitch the opening closed.

3. Machine-quilt around the outside edge and the interior of the mat. Relate your quilting lines to the printed bandanna design.

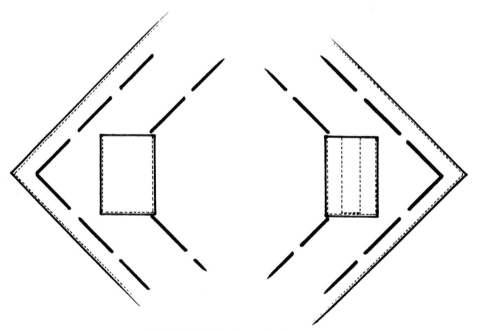

FIGURE 1. Pockets stitched to the front of a bandanna.

Barbecue Bibs

I know I'm not the only one who has trouble eating juicy hamburgers, hot dogs with all the fixings, buttered corn on the cob, and all that other good and messy barbecue food without spotting the front of whatever I'm wearing. Sometimes I joke that "I should have brought a bib!" as a cover for being a slob, but, kidding aside, I think bibs should be as common to barbecues as napkins are.

And they could be fun like the ones I made here. I picked the wildest red, white, and blue fabrics I could find and mixed them up. I even crazy-pieced scraps together for one of them.

The bibs are 13" long from neck to lower edge. The patch pockets are for paper napkins (more than one, please). After a barbecue where everyone happily dribbles, they can be tossed into the washer with a good stain-removing detergent.

MATERIALS (for each bib)

11″×18″ of a red-white-blue print, 100% cotton, for the bib
4″×4″ of a contrasting red-white-blue print for the pocket
11″×18″ of thin, soft muslin for the bib and pocket linings
24″ of white twill tape, ½″ wide
sewing thread that blends with the fabrics being stitched

DIRECTIONS

NOTE: The pattern includes a ¼″ *seam allowance*. Sew with right sides facing and edges matching.

1. Enlarge the pattern on page 63. Mark your working pattern with o's, x's, and pocket position.

2. Trace and cut out the bib and bib lining from appropriate fabrics. Cut a pocket 3½″×4½″ and a lining to match. Seam the pocket to the lining, leaving a 1½″ opening centered in one 3½″ side. After trimming corner seam allowances diagonally, turn right side out and press. Pin the pocket, opening at the bottom, to the front of the bib where the pattern indicates; edgestitch around three sides.

3. Pin one end of a 12″ length of twill tape to each x at the sides of the neck opening. With the tapes in between pinned away from the seamline, stitch the lining to the bib all around, leaving an opening between the o's. Clip the neckline seam allowance, trim the corner seam allowances diagonally, and turn right side out. Press. Edgestitch around the outside of the bib, closing the opening in the process.

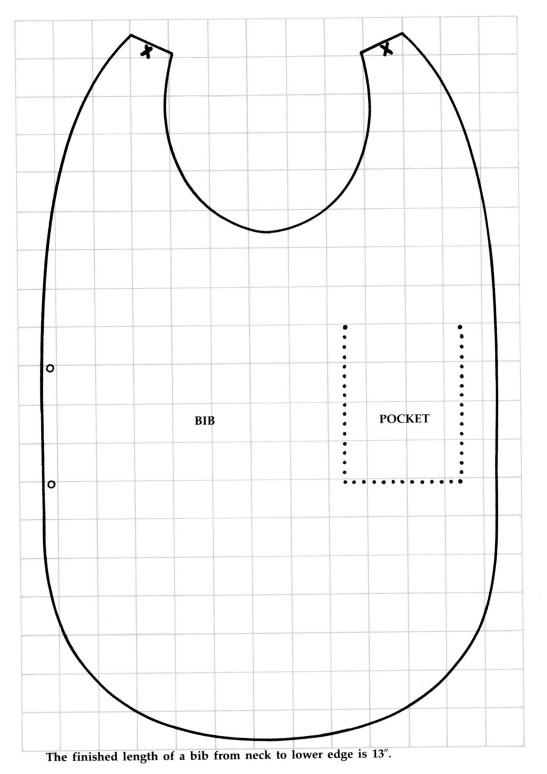

BIB

POCKET

The finished length of a bib from neck to lower edge is 13″.

1 square = 1 square inch.

A Lazy Afternoon

Summer's long, hot afternoons slow everything down. So give in. Pack your pastime portfolio with a good book and a favorite magazine; put your sunglasses, wallet, and keys in your pillow pouch; take out your siesta mat roll and get away to the beach or the park to watch the clouds roll by. A back lawn, patio, or porch will do just as well as long as everyone understands "Not to be disturbed."

Siesta Mat

To cope with what she called "the troubles," my Irish grandmother prescribed, "Lay yourself down on a bed of roses and take a nap." Remembering that advice, I used the prettiest rose-patterned fabric I could find to make this siesta mat. What could be nicer than a "Bed of Roses" for a lazy summer afternoon?

"Bed of Roses" is 72″ long by 30″ wide. Because it's constructed using an efficient, all-machine method called tunnel or channel quilting, you won't mind unrolling your "Bed of Roses" on sand or grass, or even using it as an exercise mat when summer's gone. Before you start to make it, place your sewing machine table in an unrestricted space and set up your ironing board an arm's reach away.

MATERIALS

100% cotton fabrics:
   1½ yards of a rose-patterned print for the top
   1 yard of a coordinating solid for the top
   2 yards of a print or solid for the lining
   2 yards of unbleached muslin for the interlining
   ¾ yard of a solid for the binding and tie

Other supplies:
   batting
   safety pins, size 1
   sewing thread that blends with the fabrics being stitched

DIRECTIONS

NOTE: Dimensions include a ¼" seam allowance.

1. Measure and cut the following:

Fabric	Quantity	Size
Print (top)	13	4" × 32"
Plain (top)	12	3" × 32"
Print or plain (lining)	1	
Muslin (interlining)	1	72" × 32"
Batting	1	

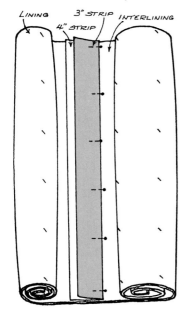

(a)

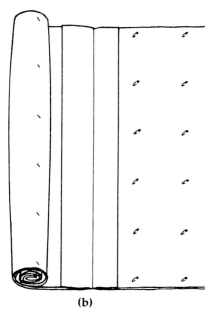

(b)

FIGURE 1. (a) Preparing to stitch the first two strips to the foundation; (b) pressing the 3″ strip to the side before proceeding to add another strip.

2. Fold the lining and interlining in half across their width and press center guideline creases. Matching these guideline creases, layer the lining, right side down, under the interlining with the batting in between. Safety-pin the layers together every 6″ to secure the foundation for working.

3. Center a 4″ print strip, right side up, over the center guideline crease in the interlining. Pin the strip to the foundation, making sure that it is straight, perpendicular to the sides, and parallel to the ends. Roll up the foundation to the left of the strip and safety-pin to secure. (**Hint:** Bicycle clips hold a quilt roll better than safety pins do.)

4. Pin a 3″ strip, right side down, to the right side of the 4″ strip, matching the edges. Rolling the foundation to the right of the pinned strips so that it will slide under the arm of the sewing machine (see Figure 1a), sew the strips together and to the foundation with the same seam. Take the foundation to the ironing board, fold the 3″ strip over to the side and press, pushing against the seam to open it fully (see Figure 1b).

5. Pin a 4″ print strip, right side down, to the right side of the 3″ strip, matching the edges. Roll, sew, and press as above. Repeat, alternating a 4″ print strip with a 3″ solid strip, until the right side of the foundation is covered with strips. As work proceeds, remove the safety pins from the foundation, adjust the roll to the left of the intended seam, and continually check for straightness. The final strip, a print, will extend over the end of the foundation.

6. Cover the other side of the foundation with strips, repeating steps 3, 4, and 5. Trim the mat to its final size, 30″×72″.

7. Cut and piece a strip 7 yards long, 3″ wide, for the binding and ties. Fold in half lengthwise, right side outside, and press. With the lining side up, sew the doubled binding around the mat ⅜″ from the matching cut edges, mitering the corners. Press the binding over the seam allowance, pushing against the seam. Turn the binding over the edge of the mat to the front. With the binding's folded edge extending 1/16″ beyond the previous seam, edgestitch the binding through all layers, mitering the corners. (**Hint:** Screw a seam-allowance gauge to the bed of your sewing machine, setting the stop slightly more than ⅜″ from the needle.) In front, the finished width of the binding will be ½″; in back, ⅜″.

8. Refold the remaining strip with right sides inside and stitch the long edges together. Turn right side out and press. Fold the seam allowances inside and edgestitch the ends. Pin the center of the tie to the center of one end of the mat on the lining side; satin-stitch across the center of the tie.

Portfolio

This is a project for you to customize. If your concept of a get-away summer afternoon involves nothing more strenuous than magazine browsing and Walkman listening with fruit for a snack and a sunblock for protection, the pockets inside the pictured portfolio will do nicely as is. But if you'd like your portfolio to accommodate your favorite needlework necessities, then revise the pocket configuration accordingly. To make your portfolio into a portable quilting center with pockets for scissors, thread, thimble, pincushion, measuring tape, patterns, patchwork pieces—whatever supplies you know you'll need—sew a number of specially sized smaller pockets to the front of the large flat pocket and, if needed, change the division and number of the pleated pockets as well.

Pleated pockets expand to hold bulky items. Small pockets can be pleated and applied over a flat pocket. Flat pockets can be layered three deep if that will help to organize more items. When opened, the inside of the portfolio measures 14″×30″, space for all kinds of handy pocket arrangements.

A closed portfolio is 14″ wide and 17″ from handles to base.

MATERIALS

100% cotton fabrics:

  10″×23″ of a print (fabric A). (For selective cutting of isolated motifs, more fabric will be needed.)

  6″×12″ of a green solid (fabric B)

  7″×14″ of a yellow solid or print (fabric C)

  6″×23″ of a red solid (fabric D)

  15″×16″ of a pink solid (fabric E)

  15″×31″ of a solid for the lining

  15″×33″ of a print for the pockets

  ½ yard of a solid for the handle holders and the binding

Other supplies:

  15″×31″ of batting

  safety pins, size 1

  15″ of twill tape, ½″ wide

  sewing thread that blends with the fabrics being stitched

  two 14½″ dowels, ½″ in diameter, for the handles

DIRECTIONS

NOTE: Patterns and dimensions include a ¼" *seam allowance.* Sew with right sides facing, edges matching, unless directed otherwise.

1. Make templates from the patterns on page 71.

2. For the patchwork (see Figure 1), cut the following:

Fabric	Pattern	Quantity	Borders
A (print)	#1	10	
	#2	8	
B (green)	#2	8	
C (yellow)	#1	8	
D (red)	#2	16	
E (pink)	#3	8	
		4	1½" × 12½"
		2	1½" × 14½"
		1	4" × 14½"

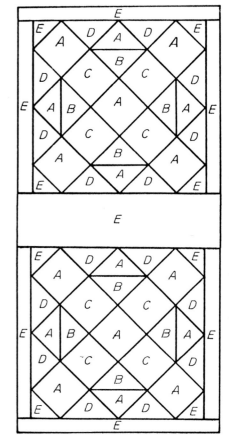

FIGURE 1. Patchwork exterior of the portfolio coded with letters that refer to the different fabrics coloring the design.

3. Piece two identical blocks, pressing the seam allowances closed after each step:

   Sew the four E corner triangles to the adjacent A squares (see Figure 2a).

   Sew four A and B triangles together into squares (see Figure 2b).

   Sew all the squares and triangles together in diagonal rows (see Figure 2c).

   Sew the rows together, pin-matching all seams that cross.

4. Seam the 12½" borders to opposite sides of each block. Sew a 1½" × 14½" border across the top of each block. To connect the blocks, sew the bottom edge of each block to a side of the 4" × 14½" border. Press these seam allowances closed.

5. Smooth the batting over the wrong side of the lining, center the patchwork over the batting (note that batting and lining are slightly larger than the patchwork), and safety-pin the layers together in the center of every square and around the borders. Working from the center out, machine-quilt each design in the ditch of every seam and across the four central squares (see Figure 3a). Trim the lining and batting to the edge of the top.

6. Cut a flat pocket 14½" × 14½". Make a 1" hem across the top. Across

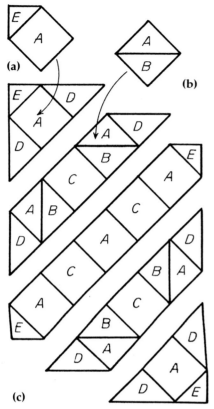

FIGURE 2. To assemble each block: (a) sew all four E triangles to A squares; (b) seam the four A and B triangles together; (c) stitch all squares and triangles together in diagonal rows and then sew the rows together.

the bottom, fold a ½" seam allowance to the back and press. Pin the pocket to the lining side of the quilted foundation, placing the hemmed top 1" from the edge of the foundation (see Figure 3b). Sewing through all layers, edgestitch the bottom of the pocket to the foundation.

7. Cut 14" × 18½" of fabric for the pleated pockets. Fold a ¼" seam allowance across one 18½" edge (the top of the pockets) to the back and press. Fold a ½" seam allowance across the opposite edge (the bottom of the pockets) to the back and press. To separate the pockets, draw a line from top to bottom 8½" from the left side. On each side of the line, form and press two pleats, each ½" deep, as Figure 3b illustrates. To hold the pleats at the top of the pockets, stitch twill tape over the seam allowance. Pin the pleated pockets to the lining side of the quilted foundation, placing the top 1" from the edge of the foundation. Sewing through all layers, edgestitch the bottom of the pocket to the foundation, securing the pleats. Starting at the bottom, backstitch by hand over the line that separates the pockets without stitching through to the front. Secure the sides of the pleated and flat pockets to the foundation by zigzag-stitching over the edges.

8. Cut four handle holders, each 4" × 10". With right sides inside, fold each holder to 4" × 5" and seam together along both 5" sides. Turn right side out and press. Make a dowel channel in each holder by turning the folded edge up 1" and zigzag-stitching over the fold. As Figure 3a illustrates, pin the holders to the front of the foundation, two at each end located 1¼" in from the foundation's sides. Secure the holders to the foundation by zigzag-stitching over the edges.

9. Cut and piece 90" of binding, 2" wide, and prepare a doubled binding. With the patchwork side of the portfolio up, sew the binding around the portfolio, stitching through all layers ¼" from the cut edges and mitering the corners. Turning the binding over the portfolio's edge to the pocket side, blindstitch the binding to the inside of the portfolio.

10. Insert the dowels into the handle-holder channels.

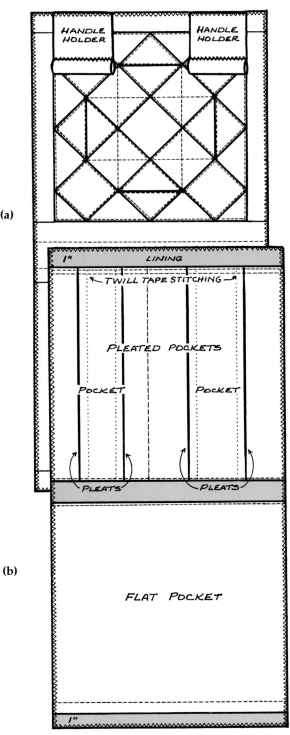

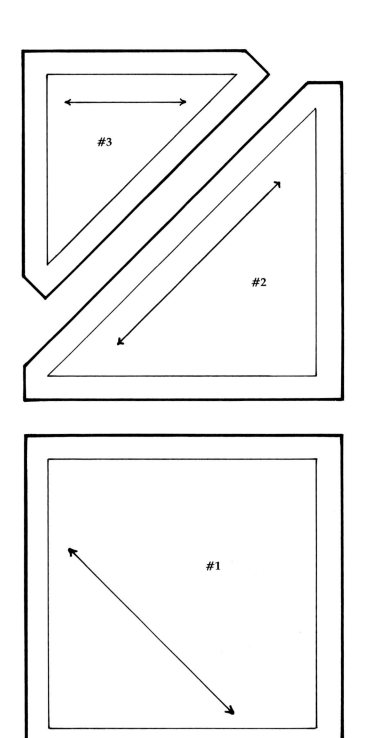

Patchwork patterns for the portfolio and the pillow pouch.

FIGURE 3. (a) Exterior and (b) interior of the portfolio prepared for binding.

Pillow Pouch

The pillow pouch, shown on page 68, has three functions. First, it's a 12″×12″ pillow; second, it's a 12″×12″ shoulder bag; and third, while you're lying on your back absorbed in the passing clouds, your wallet is safe under the pillow that cushions your head. Also, for laundering or use as a shoulder bag without the pillow, the pillow form can be removed through a zippered opening hidden inside the pouch.

The pouch combines three fabrics: two floral prints and a solid. I chose the dominant floral print first, then I looked for a secondary floral print that repeated the colors and theme in the dominant print but with lighter values. Finally, I selected a solid that united both prints by repeating a color that appears in each.

MATERIALS

100% cotton fabrics:
   13″×45″ of an allover floral print (fabric A) for the patchwork, pouch, and straps
   13″×29″ of a directional floral print (fabric B) for the patchwork and pouch lining. (For selective cutting of isolated motifs, more fabric will be needed.)
   4″×21″ of a solid for the patchwork (fabric C)
   12½″×12½″ of muslin for the interlining
   12½″×13″ of a solid for the pillow lining

Other supplies:
   12″ nylon coil zipper*
   Velcro spot fastener or large snap
   sewing thread that blends with the fabrics being stitched
   a 12″×12″ polyester-filled pillow form

   *To make a 12″ zipper from a larger zipper, measure 12″ from the top of the zipper; satin-stitch by hand or machine over the zipper coil to create a new stop; cut off the excess coil. (**HINT:** Rub a dab of white glue into the thread for strength.)

DIRECTIONS

NOTE: Patterns and dimensions include a ¼″ *seam allowance.* Sew with right sides facing, edges matching, unless directed otherwise.

1. Make templates of the patterns used for the portfolio, on page 71. Enlarge the pouch and pouch flap diagram on page 74 and make working patterns.

2. Cut the following:

Fabric	Pattern	Quantity	Straps to cut
Allover print (A)	#1	1	
	#2	8	
	#3	4	
	pouch	1	
	flap	1	
		2	2½″ × 24″
Directional print (B)	#1	4	
	#2	4	
	pouch lining	1	
	pouch flap	1	
Solid (C)	#1	4	
	#2	4	

3. Piece the pillow pouch top following the portfolio instructions on page 69, step 3, but refer to Figure 1 for positioning of the three fabrics. After pressing, machine-baste the pieced top, right side up, to the muslin interlining, stitching all sides within the seam allowance.

4. Draw a line 2″ down from one 12½″ side of the pillow lining and cut apart on that line. Turn a ¼″ seam allowance on both sides of the cut to the back and press. Attach a zipper foot to your machine. Top-stitch the folded edge of the narrow top strip of lining to the upper tape of the zipper; topstitch the folded edge of the larger piece of lining to the lower tape of the zipper. Measuring 12½″ from the top of the lining, trim the bottom edge to square the lining to 12½″ × 12½″.

5. Seam the curved edges of the pouch to the pouch lining and the pouch flap to its lining. After clipping the seam allowance of the pouch, turn both pouch and flap right side out and press. Edgestitch next to the curving seamed edges of both.

6. As Figure 2 illustrates, pin the pouch and flap, right sides up, over the zippered lining, also right side up (note the location of the zipper). Center the flap to free the ¼″ seam allowances at the sides. Machine-baste together with zigzag stitching around all sides.

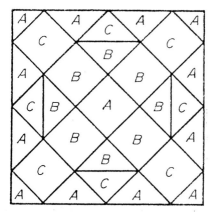

FIGURE 1. Patchwork top of the pillow pouch coded with letters that refer to the different fabrics coloring the design.

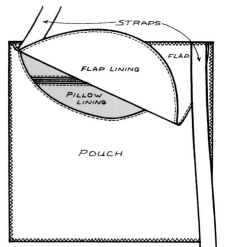

FIGURE 2. The back of the pillow pouch prepared for stitching to the patchwork top.

7. Fold each strap in half lengthwise and seam the sides and one end together. Turn right side out and press. Machine-baste the open end of each strap over the flap as Figure 2 illustrates.

8. Open the zipper. Pin the flap and straps out of the seam's way and stitch the pouch back to the pieced top around all four sides. Turn right side out through the opened zipper. Shove the pillow form into the pouch through the zipper opening.

9. To close the flap, attach a Velcro fastener or snap to flap and pouch. Tie the ends of the straps together to make a shoulder strap.

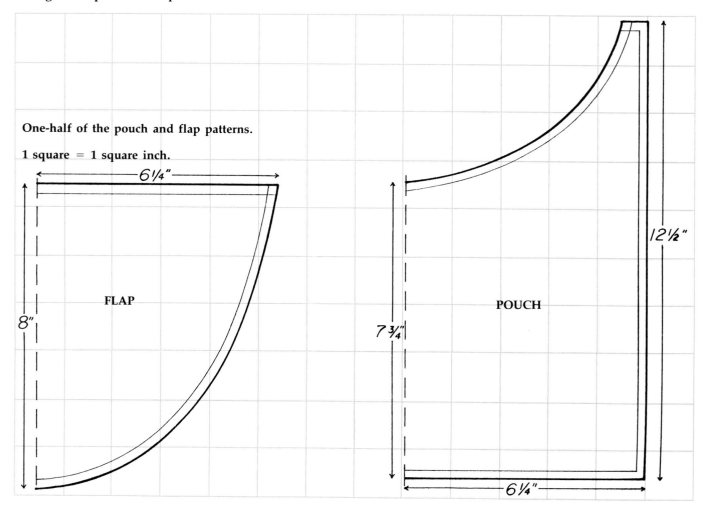

One-half of the pouch and flap patterns.

1 square = 1 square inch.

6¼"

FLAP

8"

POUCH

12½"

7¾"

6¼"

Wallet

Wrapped in America's all-time favorite fabric, this nifty little wallet has a surprise inside. Outside, it's sober, practical, durable blue denim; inside, there's a bright, flowery, lighthearted print, which also describes how you should feel when you take out your wallet to pay for something to nibble and drink on your hot, relaxing summer afternoon.

The wallet is a comfortable project for a different summer afternoon. It's easy to make, and after you've made one, you may think of other sensible but delightful combinations of fabric you can apply to wallets you can give as gifts.

MATERIALS

8″×11″ of sturdy, heavyweight blue denim for the outside

8″×11″ of a cotton print or solid for the lining

7″×20″ of a coordinating cotton print for the pockets

12″×12″ of navy blue cotton for the binding

8″×11″ of batting

a 6″ nylon coil zipper*

an adhesive-backed Velcro fastener, ⅞″ square

white thread plus thread that blends with the fabrics being stitched

a stacked insert for the cards carried in the wallet

DIRECTIONS

1. Enlarge the pattern/diagram on page 78 and cut a working pattern for the wallet.

2. Prepare the wallet foundation (see Figure 1):

   With the wrong sides facing each other, place the lining under the denim, right sides outside, and insert the batting in between. Using the width of an ordinary 12″ ruler for spacing, draw a series of parallel lines across the bias of the denim. Pinning the layers together between the lines, machine-quilt over each line with white thread and the widest zigzag stitching. Trace the outline of the wallet pattern in the center of the quilted denim and cut out.

   Centering over the x's indicated on the pattern, stick a Velcro hook square on the lining side of the flap and a Velcro loop square

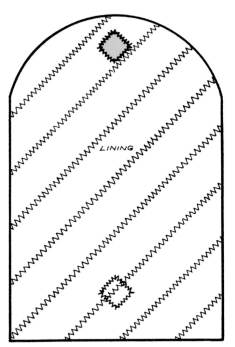

FIGURE 1. Wallet foundation, zigzag-quilted, with a Velcro fastener attached to the lining side of the flap and to the denim side at the bottom of the foundation.

*To make a 6″ zipper from a larger zipper, measure 6″ from the top of the zipper; satin-stitch by hand or machine over the zipper coil to create a new stop; cut off the excess coil. (**Hint:** Rub a dab of white glue into the thread for strength.)

75

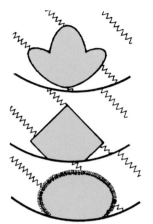

FIGURE 2. Designs appliquéd over the Velcro stitching on the denim side of the flap.

on the denim side behind the stacked insert pocket. Zigzag around each square.

To cover the Velcro stitching on the denim side of the flap, cut a small squared or rounded shape from the print pocket fabric and appliqué by hand or machine to the flap's edge (see Figure 2).

3. Make the pockets:

Cut a 6"×7" stacked insert pocket from the print fabric. Fold to 3"×7". Pin to the foundation over the lining as the diagram indicates.

Cut a 12"×7" bill and coin pocket from the print fabric. With the right side inside, seam the 7" sides together ¼" from the matched edges. Turn right side out and press the doubled pocket flat with the seam centered in back. Attach a zipper foot to your machine. Bring the bottom edge of the pocket up to the lower edge of the centered zipper; topstitch the folded edge of the pocket to the zipper's tape. Bring the top edge of the pocket down to the upper edge of the zipper, folding the pocket at the edge of the zipper's tape; topstitch the pocket to the tape, stitching through the pocket layers behind the tape as well. Pin the bill and coin pocket to the

foundation ¾" above the stacked insert. Returning to your regular presser foot, edgestitch across the bottom edge of the pocket.

Zigzag around the edge of the wallet to secure the edges of the pockets and flap appliqué and prepare for binding (see Figure 3).

4. From the binding fabric, cut and piece together about 33" of a bias strip 2" wide and prepare a doubled binding. With the denim side of the wallet up, sew the binding around the wallet ¼" from the matched cut edges. Miter the corners and ease the binding around the curve of the flap. Turning the binding over the wallet's edge to the back, blindstitch the binding to the inside of the wallet.

5. Slip the stacked insert into its pocket. (**HINT:** To hold it in place, punch two holes in the center of the plastic insert and safety-pin to the pocket through the holes.)

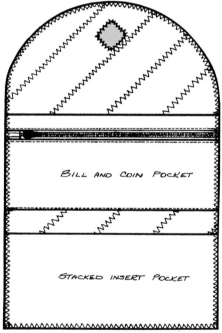

FIGURE 3. The wallet prepared for binding.

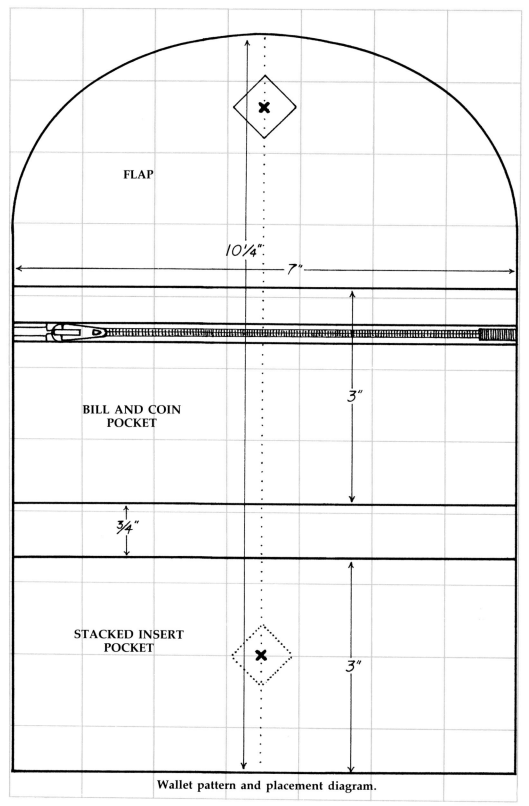

FLAP

10¼"

7"

3"

BILL AND COIN
POCKET

¾"

STACKED INSERT
POCKET

3"

Wallet pattern and placement diagram.

1 square = 1 square inch.

Glasses Case

In the brilliant sun of a summer afternoon, sunglasses are a necessity. The soft eyeglasses case pictured on page 76 has a hidden asset, an inside pocket for a packet of lens tissues or a handkerchief. Make the eyeglasses case to match your wallet.

MATERIALS

8″×8″ of sturdy, heavyweight denim for the outside

8″×8″ of thin muslin for the interlining

8″×8″ of a cotton print for the lining

3½″×4″ of a cotton print or solid for the pocket

8″×8″ of batting

white sewing thread and thread that blends with the other fabrics being stitched

DIRECTIONS

NOTE: Pattern and dimensions include a ¼″ *seam allowance*. Sew with right sides facing and edges matching.

1. Make a full-size copy of the pattern on page 80.

2. Layer the denim, right side up, over the muslin interlining with the batting in between. Using the width of an ordinary 12″ ruler for spacing, draw a series of parallel lines across the bias of the denim. Pinning the layers together between the lines, machine-quilt over each line with white thread and the widest zigzag stitching. Trace the pattern's outline on the center of the quilted denim and cut out.

3. Trace and cut a pattern piece from the lining, marking ● 's on the wrong side. Turn the seam allowances around both 4″ and one 3½″ sides of the pocket to the back and press; make a 1″ hem across the remaining side, the top of the pocket. Edgestitch the pocket to the right side of the lining where the pattern indicates (see Figure 1).

4. Sew the lining to the quilted denim at the top from ● to ● . Clip the seam allowance to the stitching at each ●, trim ⅛″ from the seam and turn right side out. With the denim inside, fold the case in half, matching the ● 's; sew from the fold to the corner, pivot, and sew to the ● . Trim the seam allowance ⅛″ from the seam and zigzag over the seam allowance. Turn right side out. With doubled thread, sew six satin stitches across the seam at ● to strengthen the opening.

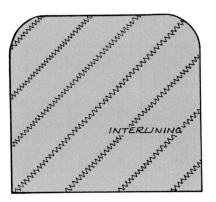

(a)

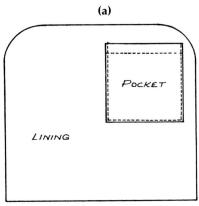

(b)

FIGURE 1. (a) Quilted denim and (b) lining with pocket before stitching together into the eyeglasses case.

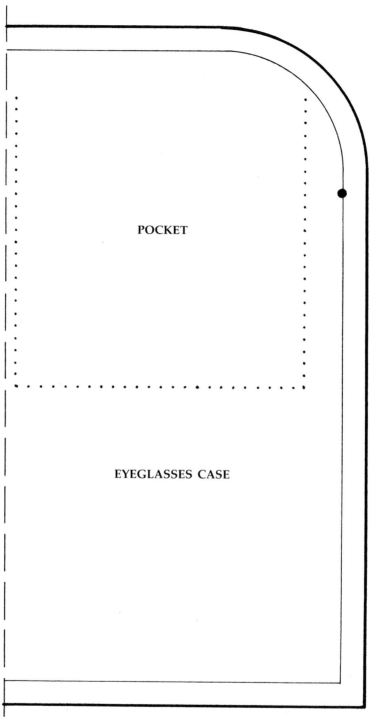

POCKET

EYEGLASSES CASE

One-half of the eyeglasses case pattern.

Daisylou and Poppy

Returning home from Sunday school, Poppy and Daisy-lou like to stop at the little park they pass on the way. They take off their shoes and socks for a run through the grass and then they sit by the pond, where they feed a group of ducks whose antics, as they dash, dive, splash, and quack after the crumbs, they delight in watching.

Three-Dimensional Doll

"What's a doll doing in my quilting book?" you have every right to ask. I've taken sneaky advantage of the opportunity in order to introduce a needlecraft that utilizes materials and methods you'll find familiar, while adding a few procedures that are new to create cloth figures that will complement the quilted items you make. Daisylou and Poppy, 14" tall, with movable arms and legs and removable dresses and panties, can be soft sculptures to display with your quilts or play dolls for a child.

Precision sewing is as important to dollmaking as it is to piecing a patchwork top but, because doll patterns are curvier, slower stitching is the norm, with frequent stops to reposition a convoluted seam-in-progress under the presser foot. Stuffing is the critical process that separates dollmaking from quiltmaking, and that's the challenge of this project.

MATERIALS (for one doll)

11" × 29" of flesh-colored 100% cotton for the body

polyester stuffing

a scrap of white press-on mending tape for the eyes

a blue or brown felt-tip pen for coloring the eyes

brown or black embroidery floss for eye outlines and rosy pink or deep red floss for the mouth

3 oz. of brown or black 3- or 4-ply acrylic yarn for the wig

7½" × 21" of a cotton print for the dress skirt

8" × 10" of a coordinating cotton solid for the dress bodice

9" × 9" of thin white or pink cotton for the panties

22" of flat eyelet or ruffled lace for dress trim

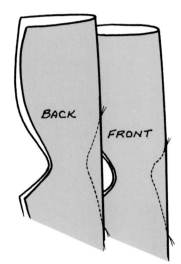

FIGURE 1. Stitching a long dart into the body back and a shorter dart into the front.

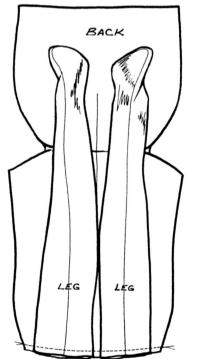

FIGURE 2. Machine-basting the legs to the body.

30″ of elastic, ⅛″ wide, for the panties

two small snaps and three tiny buttons for the dress

sewing thread that matches the body fabric, the wig yarn, and the dress fabrics

ribbon for a hair bow

DIRECTIONS

NOTE: Patterns (except for the arm and leg patterns) and dimensions include a ¼″ *seam allowance*. Sew with right sides facing, edges matching, unless directed otherwise.

1. Make working copies of the patterns on pages 86 and 87.

2. From the body fabric, trace and cut a body front and body back, marking the appropriate dart stitching lines on the reverse sides. Turn the top-of-the-head seam allowances to the back and press. With tiny machine stitching, fold and sew the vertical darts into the front and back (see Figure 1), trim the seam allowances ⅛″ from the stitching, and clip the deepest parts of the curves. Fold and sew the horizontal darts, stitching across the vertical darts.

3. Trace the outlines of the leg pattern twice onto doubled body fabric, keeping the outlines ½″ apart. Stitch over the outlines, leaving the tops and stuffing openings unseamed. Stitch again around the foot and ankle curves. Cut out ¼″ outside the seams, clip the seam allowances at the ankle curves, and turn the legs right side out.

4. Laying the legs side by side, feet pointing up, over the right side of the body back, machine-baste the top of the legs to the hip edge of the back, keeping the legs inside the body's side seam allowances (see Figure 2). Safety-pin the legs together at the ankles.

5. With right sides together and the legs in between, pin and sew the body front to the back, leaving the top of the head unseamed. (HINT: Sew in sections, hip seam first, then side-of-torso seams, and finally side-of-head and neck seams.) Stitch again over the side-of-head and neck seams. Clip the seam allowances at the side of the neck and, grasping the feet, pull the body right side out.

6. Stuff the body and legs firmly. Turn the casing often and frequently hold the developing figure at arm's length to check for symmetry:

    Using a tool to shove wads of stuffing through the head opening into the lower cavity, fill the torso tightly, compressing the stuffing into a smooth, dense mass. After the shoulders and chest have been stuffed to capacity, pack the crucial neck area with stuffing,

FIGURE 3. Stuffed torso and head with movable arms attached by hand stitching.

FIGURE 4. Exact-size eye patterns.

FIGURE 5. Outline stitching used when embroidering the mouth and around the eye circles.

blending stuffing down into the chest stuffing. Stuff the lower half of the head, blending this stuffing with the neck stuffing. Model a chin from the inside with stuffing placement and directional force. Before proceeding further, hand-sew running stitches next to the folded edge around the top opening using quadrupled thread and leaving long tails at the ends of the seam. Stuff the top of the head, draw up the thread to gather the top around the stuffing, add more stuffing, draw up the thread again and, when the opening is about as big as your little finger, tie the thread tails to secure. Force more stuffing through the opening into the head, working out any wrinkles that may have strayed too far down into the forehead area. Finish shaping the head and torso with hand and finger pressure, smoothing and modeling as if the figure were made of clay.

Tack a circle of body fabric about 1½" in diameter over the opening at the top of the head (see Figure 3).

Bracing the torso upside down between your knees, stuff the legs firmly to the kneeline and moderately firm above; allow stuffing to become cushiony just before joining the hip. Turning the seam allowances inside, ladder-stitch the openings closed.

7. Trace the outlines of the arm pattern twice onto doubled body fabric, keeping the outlines ¼" apart. Stitch over the outlines, leaving the tops open. Cut out ⅛" outside the seams, clip the seam allowances at the wrist-thumb curves, and turn right side out. Stuff the arms firmly to the elbows, reducing gradually to soft at the top. Turning the seam allowances inside, overcast and gather the top openings closed, tacking the corners together. To attach each arm with thumb pointing forward, run a double-threaded needle through the shoulder point, through the top of the arm, into the shoulder and through the arm again, working the needle between the two about ten times to create a strong, tight connection before securing the thread (see Figure 3). (HINT: A rubber finger or pliers helps to pull the needle out of tight places.)

8. Duplicating the circles in Figure 4, trace and cut two eyes from white press-on mending tape. Color the irises with a felt-tip pen. Pin to the head (the eyeline is halfway between the neck dart and the top of the head) and fuse with the tip of a hot iron. With two strands of brown or black floss, embroider around each eye with outline stitching (see Figure 5) and add eyelashes with single stitches. Pencil a curving mouth line using a large thread spool as a template. Outline-stitch with two strands of pink or red floss, adding shorter rows of adjacent stitching underneath for thickness. Tint the cheeks of a light-skinned doll with blusher.

9. Using pinheads as markers, define a hairline that runs from eyeline to eyeline and frames the face nicely (see Figure 6). Cutting strands of yarn 28″ long as needed, fold the yarn in half, three strands at a time, and stitch to the hairline, sewing twice over the center loop of the yarn with doubled thread (see Figure 7). After covering the hairline completely with yarn, smooth the strands back to the nape of the neck and hold them temporarily with a rubber band around the neck. With large, tight backstitches, sew the yarn to the back of the head ½″ above the rubber band. Remove the rubber band, bring the yarn up over itself to the top of the head, and bind and tie the ends together with another strand of yarn. Tack the binding yarn securely to the head. Trim and brush out the ends of the yarn. Make a bow and tack to the head.

FIGURE 6. Heads with facial features applied and hairlines marked with pins.

10. For the dress, trace and cut two bodice backs from doubled fabric, one bodice front on the fold of doubled fabric, and one facing. Pressing after each step:

   Sew the bodice front to the backs at the shoulders, clipping the seam allowances at the curves. Press and stitch a narrow hem into the edge of each sleeve.

   Matching ▼ 's, sew the sides of the front facing to the back facings. Matching all ▼ 's and shoulder seams, sew the facing around the neck (see Figure 8). Trim the seam allowance ⅛″ from the seam, clip, and turn right side out.

   Sew the front to the back at the sides, clipping the seam allowances under arms.

   Turning the side seam allowances to the back, gather the 21″ width of the skirt to 10″. Distributing the gathers evenly, sew the skirt to the bodice. Measuring from the lower edge, sew the sides of the skirt together for 5″. Fold and press a ½″ hem; sew the hem and catch the top of the lace over the hem with the same seam.

   Attach two snaps to close the bodice in back and sew three buttons in a row to the bodice center front.

FIGURE 7. Stitching yarn to the head.

11. Trace and cut two panty sides on the fold of doubled fabric. Matching ▼ 's, sew the sides together down the center front and clip the seam allowance at the curve. Turn the waist and leg seam allowances to the back and press. Measure and pencil-mark 7″ of elastic. Tacking at the start, place the elastic on top of the waist seam allowance and zigzag a thread channel over it; pull the elastic until the 7″ mark appears, cut at that point, and secure the end. Repeat on each leg with 3½″ lengths of elastic. Sew the sides together down the center back, clipping the curving seam allowance. Matching the center seams, stitch the legs together.

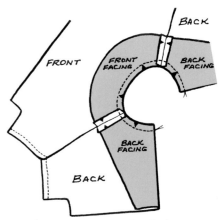

FIGURE 8. Sewing the facing around the neck of the dress bodice.

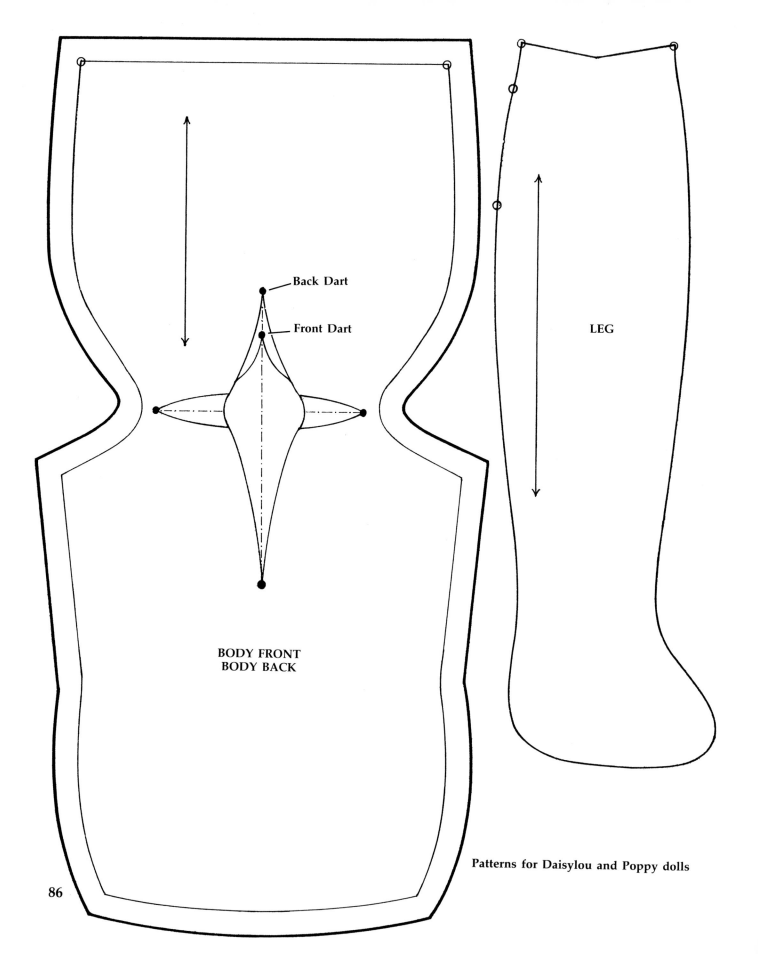

Back Dart

Front Dart

**BODY FRONT
BODY BACK**

LEG

Patterns for Daisylou and Poppy dolls

86

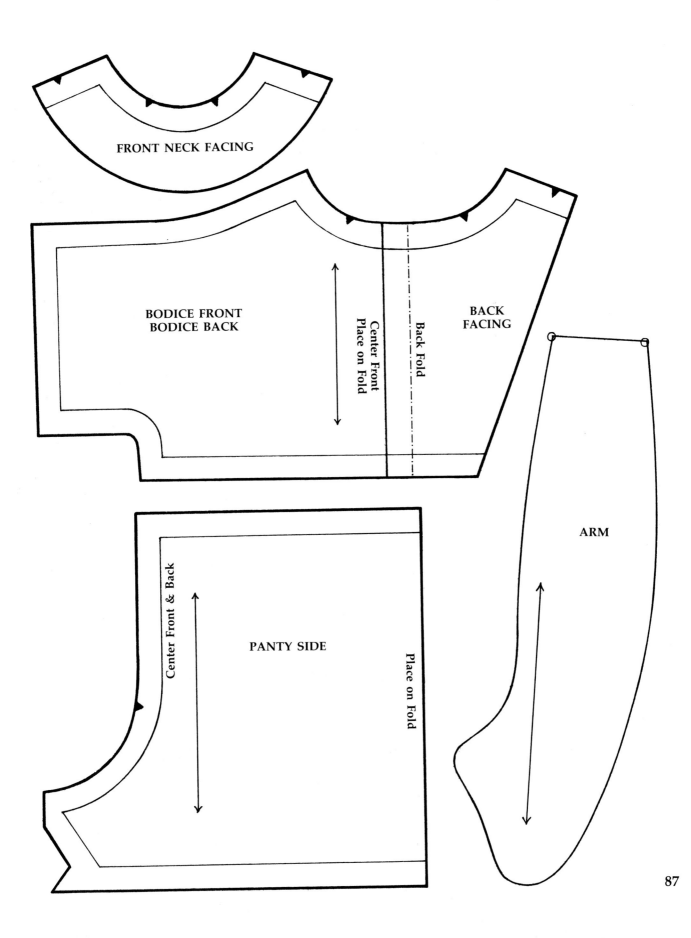

FRONT NECK FACING

BODICE FRONT
BODICE BACK

Center Front
Place on Fold

Back Fold

BACK
FACING

ARM

Center Front & Back

PANTY SIDE

Place on Fold

87

Fall

Fall deepens summer's colors and then lets them go. The hazy tones of purple, red, orange, brown, green, and gold that enrich the landscape fade as the weather changes from cool to cold.

In this section, you're invited to run through the fallen leaves, bewitch the children, and bring a harvest of the season's colors indoors for Thanksgiving.

Instructions for the *Fall* panel start on page 17.

Jogger's Fall

When the weather grows chilly and the foliage begins to turn, joggers are in their element. Even people like me, who much prefer indoor exercise, love to get out there and walk, enjoying the colors, the crisp air, and the crunchy leaves underfoot. Whether jogging or walking, a sweatshirt and earmuffs are comfortable items to wear, protection against those penetrating gusts of wind that suddenly erupt at this time of the year. The "designer" sweatshirt and earmuffs that follow provide the necessary insulation, together with a dash of seasonal style.

Sweatshirt

I've read instructions for appliquéing on sweatshirts that began, "Remove neckband." Maneuvering a bulky sweatshirt to position a shoulder appliqué under the sewing machine's presser foot requires firm management, but the passing inconvenience is better than taking off the neckband and putting it back on again, to my way of working. Besides, appliqués stabilized with transfer web resist tugging and pulling to stay in shape.

Although you can't see the back of my sweatshirt, there are a few leaves scattered over the shoulder, an option I leave to your improvisation. Before you start to sew, wash a new sweatshirt and fill a bobbin for each spool of thread you'll be using. And beware of stitching the back to the front of the sweatshirt in tricky places!

MATERIALS

one sweatshirt

scraps of print and plain cotton fabric in coordinating fall colors for the leaf appliqués

12″ of Pellon Wonder-Under™ transfer web

16 safety pins, size 1

sewing thread in colors that accent the fabrics being machine-appliquéd

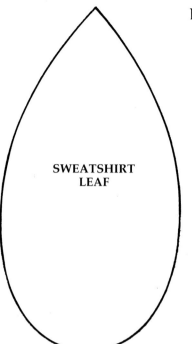

**SWEATSHIRT
LEAF**

DIRECTIONS

1. Make a template of the leaf pattern.

2. Trace the leaf sixteen times onto the paper backing of the transfer web, spacing the outlines ¼" apart. Pinning the web to the paper, rough-cut each leaf ⅛" from the outline. With a hot iron, fuse the transfer-web leaf to the reverse side of a scrap of leaf fabric. When cool, cut out on the outline and remove the paper.

3. Referring to the design in Figure 1, arrange the leaves on the front of the sweatshirt and safety-pin in place. Starting at the shoulder, unpin, fuse, and machine-appliqué the leaves in order as they are numbered in the design. Pin overlapping leaves out of the way. Begin with narrow satin stitching at the tip of a leaf; gradually step up to wider satin stitching around the lower half of the leaf, and resume narrow satin stitching at the return to the tip. Pivot at the tip and satin-stitch a vein down the center of the leaf, increasing the stitch width bit by bit. Extend the vein beyond the base of the leaf into a short stem (see Figure 2). Note that the portion of a leaf covered by another leaf doesn't need satin stitching.

FIGURE 1. Leafy sweatshirt design with the leaves numbered in appliqué order.

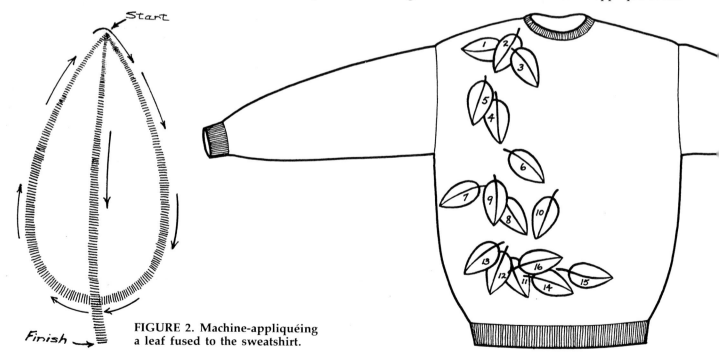

FIGURE 2. Machine-appliquéing a leaf fused to the sweatshirt.

Earmuffs

In ancient Greece, a victorious runner was crowned with a circlet of laurel leaves. Stretch your imagination and think of these earmuffs as your "crown of laurels." You might decide to limit the patchwork leaf trim you apply to clusters over the earmuffs, as I did in my example, pictured on page 94, or you can go for a full coronet of leaves around your head. You'll be a winner either way.

MATERIALS

a pair of earmuffs

a 30" strip of cotton fabric, 2½" wide, to cover the headband

scraps at least 3½" square of print and plain cotton fabric in coordinating fall colors for the leaves

Pellon Wonder-Under™ transfer web

pipe cleaners 6" long

sewing thread in colors that accent the fabrics being satin-stitched

DIRECTIONS

1. Make a template of the leaf pattern on page 94.

2. Turn a ¼" seam allowance on all sides of the 30" × 2½" strip to the back and press. With the right side outside, fold the strip around the plastic headband between the earmuffs; overcast the folded edges together, encasing the headband inside a loosely fitted, gathered tube of fabric. Gather the ends of the tube tightly around the ends of the headband where it joins the muffs.

3. Make as many patchwork leaf trims as desired (see Figure 1):

   For each leaf, cut fabric 3½" square and transfer fuse 3½" × 1¾". With the right side outside, fold and press the fabric square in half, insert the transfer fuse inside, and press with a hot iron to fuse. Open and remove the paper backing.

   Trim a pipe cleaner to 5½". Make two pencil marks on the pipe cleaner, each 2½" from an end. Center the pipe cleaner inside the folded fabric, matching a pencil mark to the edge of the fabric. Press, fusing the fabric around the pipe cleaner. Repeat, fusing another square of folded fabric around the other end of the pipe cleaner.

   Trace leaf outlines onto the fabric (the pipe cleaner will be the center vein). Satin-stitch as instructed for the sweatshirt in step 3 on page 92, but satin-stitch over the pipe cleaner to define the vein

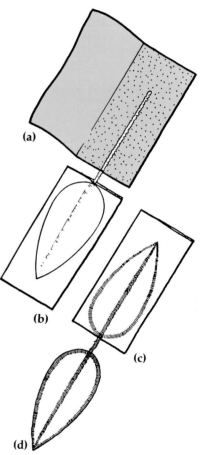

FIGURE 1. To make a patchwork leaf trim: (a) center a pipe cleaner inside folded fabric prepared with transfer fuse; (b) after fusing the fabric around the pipe cleaner, trace a leaf outline; (c) satin-stitch over the outline and pipe cleaner vein of both leaves; (d) cut out the leaves.

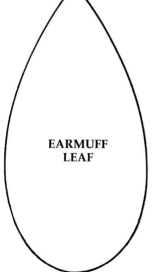

**EARMUFF
LEAF**

and continue on to the tip of the opposite leaf; pivot and satin-stitch that leaf's outline. (**HINT:** Use a presser foot with a grooved base that allows for the thickness of the pipe cleaner.)

With a small scissors, cut out the leaves, carefully following the outside needle holes without snipping a thread.

4. Laying the patchwork leaf trims across the headband, tack each trim to the fabric covering the headband, sewing over the pipe cleaner between the leaves. Arrange the leaves to frame the head attractively.

The Witches of Brew

When the kids return from trick-or-treat on Halloween, meet them with mugs of hot chocolate or cider and tell them about the Witches of Brew . . . who live in a castle built of broken pottery . . . located next to a fallen log by a freshwater spring hidden deep in the heart of the forest . . . who emerge on nights when the moon is full to search under fallen leaves for tiny mushrooms that glow silvery in the dark . . . which they slice and chop and stew and stir while they sing and chatter and chant . . . and the potion they brew is magical stuff only for children who dream when they sleep . . . about little witches who carry spoons and live in a castle built of broken pottery located next to a fallen log in the forest. . . .

Mug Cozy

When Halloween is over, you can use the quilted skirt of a witch as a cozy over the mug of coffee or tea you sip while you're sewing. The witchy head can be removed for safekeeping until next Halloween.

MATERIALS

½ yard of 100% cotton black print for the skirt and neck ruffle
⅓ yard of 100% cotton unbleached muslin for the skirt lining and the head
scraps of red and black press-on mending tape for the facial features
5″ × 9″ of black felt for the hat
a scrap of orange felt or bias tape for the hatband
8″ × 16″ of batting
polyester stuffing
black yarn
sewing thread to match the fabrics being stitched
two large safety pins
1 plastic spoon

DIRECTIONS

Note: Patterns (except for the head and arms) and dimensions include a ¼" *seam allowance*. Sew with right sides facing, edges matching, unless directed otherwise.

1. Make copies of the patterns on page 99.

2. Cut a 12" × 16" skirt from the black print and an 8" × 16" skirt lining from the muslin. With the batting on top of the lining, sew the skirt to the lining/batting along both 16" edges. Trim the batting from both seam allowances. Turn right side out, folding along one of the seams. Press the other seam and the doubled skirt fabric above it, the neck ruffle, flat.

3. Starting 1½" from one side, mark fourteen vertical lines 1" apart on the lining. Machine-quilt over each line. Do not quilt the neck ruffle (see Figure 1a).

4. Fold and stitch the sides of the skirt and neck ruffle together through all layers except the ruffle/lining/batting layer on the top, which should be pushed away from the seamline. Flatten the tubular skirt/ruffle, centering the seam. After trimming the batting overlap, fold the seam allowance on the loose ruffle/lining edge to the inside and blindstitch over the seam (see Figure 1b).

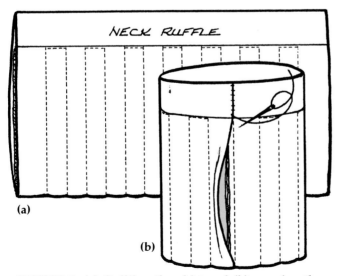

(a)

(b)

FIGURE 1. (a) Quilting the skirt and (b) seaming the sides together quilt-as-you-go style.

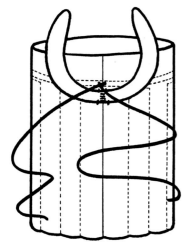

FIGURE 2. Drawstring inserted and arms attached to the skirt.

FIGURE 3. Tacking strands of yarn to the head.

5. Stitch two parallel seams ¼″ apart around the base of the neck ruffle just above the lining. Turn the skirt/ruffle right side out. Thread a blunt needle with yarn. Work a doubled yarn drawstring into and through the ¼″ channel, bringing the ends of the drawstring out on either side of the joining seam.

6. Trace the arm pattern onto the wrong side of a piece of doubled black fabric. Sew over the traced outline, leaving an opening between the o's. Cut out ⅛″ outside the seamline. Clip the inside seam allowance, turn right side out, and ladder-stitch the opening closed. Tack the center of the arms, facing up, to the skirt as Figure 2 illustrates.

7. Trace the head pattern onto a piece of doubled unbleached muslin. Sew over the traced outline, leaving the top open. Cut out ¼″ outside the seamline and top, clip the seam allowance at the angles, and turn right side out. Stuff firmly. Folding the top seam allowance inside, hand-sew running stitches next to the fold and gather tightly around full stuffing. Add more stuffing through the hole. Cut two eyes from black and a mouth from red press-on tape. (**HINT:** These don't have to be cut perfectly to be fun.) Fuse to the head with the tip of a hot iron. Cut strands of black yarn 2″ to 4″ long. Tack the strands to the head two at a time, backstitching over the center of the strands (see Figure 3). Ring the head with scraggly yarn that will stick out from underneath the hat.

8. Cut a hat crown and brim from black felt. Fold and stitch the sides of the crown together, trim next to the seam, and turn right side out. Clip the inner seam allowance of the brim every ¼″. Sew the crown to the brim and trim next to the seam (see Figure 4). Stuff the crown of the hat softly. Pin the hat to the head and attach with backstitches over the seam. Tack a hatband of orange felt or bias tape around the base of the crown.

9. Gather the skirt around the neck of the head; wrap and tie the drawstring snugly. Underneath the skirt, run two safety pins through the neck stump to hold the head in place. Overlap the hands ¾″, tacking the tips. Slip the handle of a plastic spoon through the tacked hands.

FIGURE 4. Preparing to seam the hat crown to the brim.

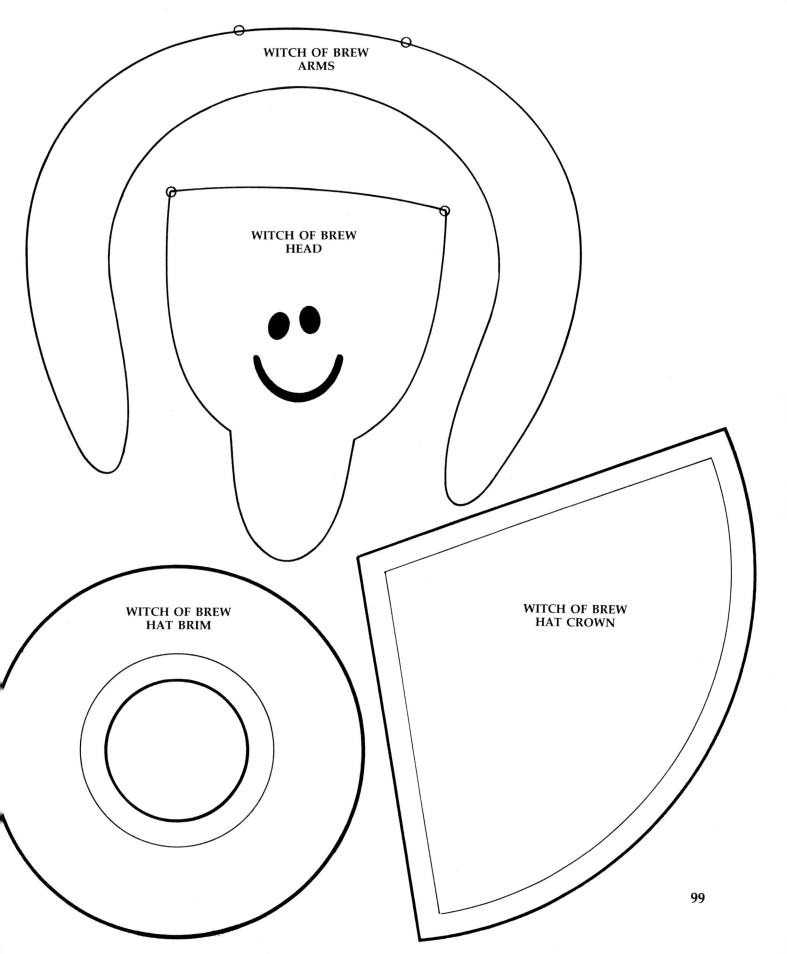

WITCH OF BREW
ARMS

WITCH OF BREW
HEAD

WITCH OF BREW
HAT BRIM

WITCH OF BREW
HAT CROWN

99

An Autumn Table Setting

I have a friend who starts to decorate her home for the end-of-year holidays a week before Thanksgiving. Every year she covers her dining-room table with a gorgeous textile she bought on a trip to Morocco and arranges a harvest centerpiece to set it off. The centerpiece changes character as the weeks advance toward the 25th of December, but the tablecloth, a family tradition, remains. I'm not sure that she serves Thanksgiving dinner on that tablecloth, but I know she uses it for informal entertaining.

Tablecloth and Napkins

If you can't get to Morocco to find an exotic covering for your festive table, you can make this unusual and ornamental tablecloth with yo-yos—or Suffolk puffs, the mellower name by which yo-yos are known in Britain. When gathered puffs are combined with rectangles of smooth fabric, the result is very different from the conventional yo-yo bedspread quilters know. It also takes less time to make!

The tablecloth I made consists of four modular sections that combine to a size of 62″ × 74″. Because the design is sectional and each section can also be reduced or expanded, you can make your tablecloth larger or smaller if you choose.

Each of the six yo-yo–accented napkins is a dinner-size 18″ square.

MATERIALS

6 yards of 100% cotton print fabric, 45″ wide, for tablecloth rectangles and six napkins

7½ yards of 100% cotton coordinating solid fabric, 45″ wide, for yo-yos and linings

matching sewing thread

DIRECTIONS

1. Make templates of the corner and yo-yo patterns on page 104.
2. Cut the following:

Pattern Piece	Fabric	Quantity	Size	Size after Sewing
Rectangle A	print solid	4 4	7″ × 19″	6″ × 18″
Rectangle B	print solid	4 4	7″ × 9″	6″ × 8″
Rectangle C	print solid	4 4	15″ × 13″	14″ × 12″
Rectangle D	print solid	4 4	15″ × 27″	14″ × 26″
Rectangle E	print solid	4 4	11″ × 5″	10″ × 4″
Rectangle F	print solid	4 4	11″ × 7″	10″ × 6″
Yo-yo	solid	367*	pattern	2″ diameter
Napkin	print	6	19″ × 19″	18″ × 18″

*361 for the tablecloth; 6 for the napkins

Refer to the layout in Figure 1 when cutting the rectangles.

3. With right sides together and edges matching, pin each print rectangle to its corresponding solid lining rectangle. Using the corner shaper, round off the four corners of each rectangle. Machine-stitch ½″ from the cut edges, leaving a 2″ opening on one of the short sides. Trim the seam allowances around the corner curves to ⅛″, turn right side out, and press. Ladder-stitch the openings closed. Topstitch each rectangle 1″ from the outside edge, then set your machine for narrow satin stitching and satin-stitch over the straight-stitched seam.

FIGURE 1. Layout for cutting tablecloth rectangles (top and lining) from fabric 45″ wide.

4. To make each of the 361 tablecloth yo-yos: Turning under the ¼″ seam allowance ahead of the needle, hand-sew around the circle next to the folded edge with doubled thread and running stitches ³⁄₁₆″ wide; gather tightly and secure the thread. Flatten the yo-yo, centering the gathered hole (see Figure 2).

5. Following the diagram on page 105, construct the tablecloth. Working with right sides facing (the gathered side of a yo-yo is its right side), tack the yo-yos together (see Figure 3) into rows and then tack the rows to the rectangles as described below, overcasting the edges where they meet for ⅜″. To assemble each of the four tablecloth sections:

> Make a row of five yo-yos and tack between rectangles E and F.
>
> Make a row of six yo-yos and tack between unit E + F and rectangle C.
>
> Make a row of thirteen yo-yos and tack between unit E + F + C and rectangle D.
>
> Make a row of three yo-yos and tack between rectangles A and B.

As the diagram on page 105 indicates, connect the four sections with yo-yo rows (note how the sections are turned) and finish the tablecloth with a yo-yo border.

6. Make ½″ hems on all sides of each 19″ square of fabric. Trace the topstitching seamline indicated on the yo-yo pattern onto the wrong sides of six yo-yo circles. With right sides together, match and pin one circle to one corner of each napkin and machine-stitch around the inner seamline. Proceed to gather each circle into a yo-yo as described in step 4 (see Figure 4).

FIGURE 2. Making a yo-yo.

FIGURE 3. Tacking yo-yos together.

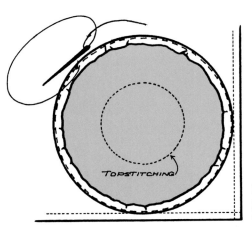

TOPSTITCHING

FIGURE 4. Making a yo-yo previously seamed to the corner of a napkin.

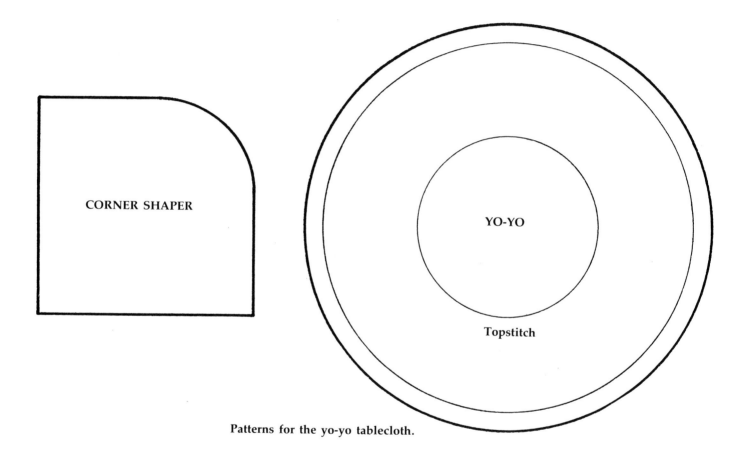

CORNER SHAPER

YO-YO

Topstitch

Patterns for the yo-yo tablecloth.

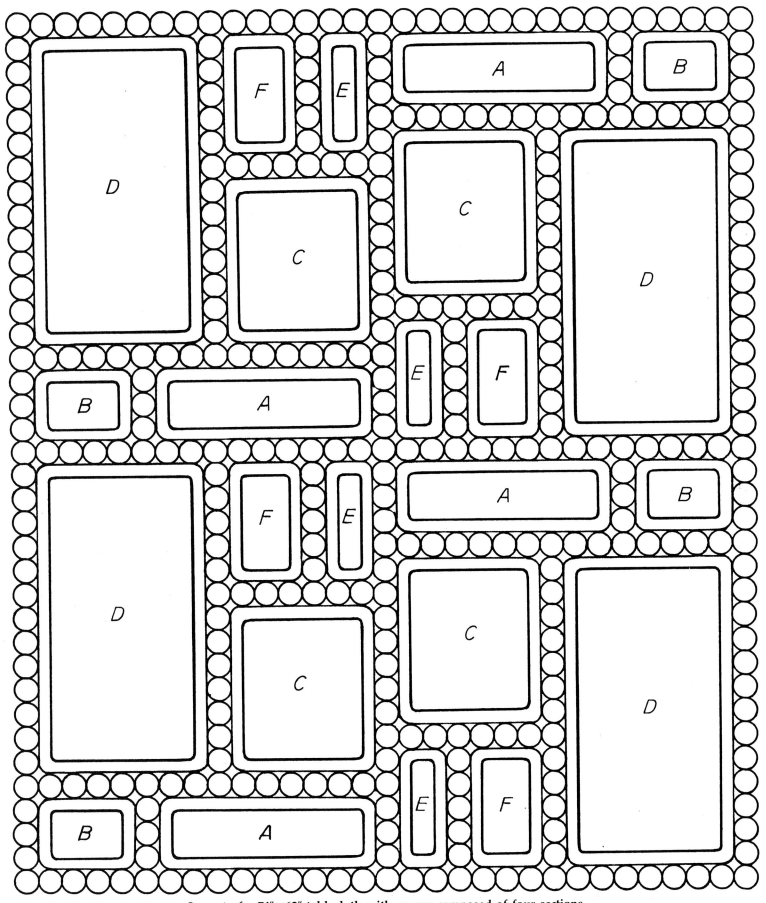

Layout of a 74″ × 62″ tablecloth with yo-yos composed of four sections, with the two left-hand sections rotated on the right side.

Yo-Yo Flowers

While I was working on the yo-yo tablecloth (pictured on page 101), these yo-yo flowers begged to be made. I especially like the way they make use of both the right and wrong sides of print fabric.

If you can't find florists' wire, you can substitute long pipe cleaners or lengths of wooden dowel ⅛" in diameter with a drop of white glue to anchor the yo-yos.

MATERIALS

pieces of cotton prints and solids at least 6" square
florists' wire cut into 14" lengths
sewing thread
batting scraps and stuffing

DIRECTIONS

1. Make a template of the yo-yo flower pattern.

2. Trace and cut out the yo-yo circles.

3. Trace an inner gathering line onto the wrong side of each circle. Using doubled thread, sew running stitches around the gathering line. Bend the tip of a length of florists' wire into a loop by wrapping it around a pencil (see Figure 1a). Encase the wire loop inside a ball of stuffing topped with a scrap of batting; insert under the yo-yo circle and gather the stitches tightly around the stuffing and batting (see Figure 1b). Add more stuffing if needed, then wrap the sewing thread around the base of the ball and secure.

4. Folding the outer seam allowance to the inside, sew running stitches ³⁄₁₆" wide next to the folded edge of the circle. Gather tightly around the base of the center ball and secure the thread.

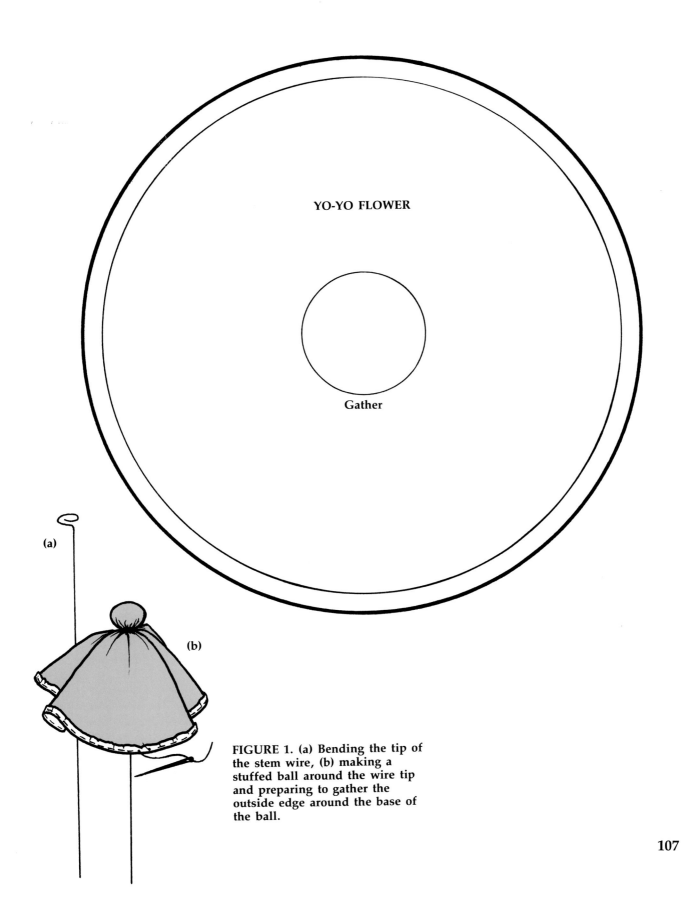

YO-YO FLOWER

Gather

(a)

(b)

FIGURE 1. (a) Bending the tip of the stem wire, (b) making a stuffed ball around the wire tip and preparing to gather the outside edge around the base of the ball.

The Decorative but Practical Hostess

Hostessing a Thanksgiving feast is a very nitty-gritty business, particularly if the hostess is also the cook. It's the kind of event that takes utilitarian accessories generally relegated to the kitchen into the dining room. To live up to the change of scene, aprons and potholders undergo a makeover.

Apron

For serious cooking, I'm generally in old jeans and stained T-shirts, but for serious serving, I want an apron to protect my hostessy attire—not one of those little frilly jobs, but something functional that's also attractive, like this ample-skirted apron with the openwork border of inserted yo-yos. It's pretty enough to be expanded into part of a country-style outfit, becoming the overskirt on top of an underskirt of contrasting color.

To alter the apron's 26½" length, add or subtract to the skirt at the waist. To change the width of the skirt, add or subtract in increments of 2" (equal to the diameter of a yo-yo), and adjust the size of the waistband.

MATERIALS

1½ yards of a 100% cotton solid, 45" wide
matching sewing thread

DIRECTIONS

NOTE: Dimensions include a ½" *seam allowance.* Sew with right sides facing, edges matching, unless directed otherwise.

---

1. Make a template of the tablecloth yo-yo pattern on page 104.
2. Following the cutting guide (see Figure 1), measure and cut the following:

Pattern Piece	Quantity	Size
Border	1	9" × 43"
Skirt	1	22" × 44"
Pocket	1	7" × 8"
Waistband	1	3½" × 24"
Tie	2	3½" × 22"
Yo-yo	23*	pattern

*22 for the skirt, 1 for the pocket.

3. Folding the border in half lengthwise, sew the three cut sides together, leaving a 3" opening in the center of the long side. Turn right side out and press. Ladder-stitch the opening closed. (Size after sewing: 4" × 42".)

4. Press and stitch 1" hems into the two short sides and the bottom edge of the skirt. (Size after hemming: 21" × 42".)

5. Fold the seam allowances on both 8" sides and one 7" side of the pocket to the back and press. Make a 1" hem along the top of the pocket. Attach a yo-yo to the inner corner just below the hem (follow the method used for the napkins described on page 103, step 6.) Pin the pocket to the right side of the skirt 6" from the top, 9" from the side, and edgestitch to the skirt.

6. Make twenty-two yo-yos (follow the yo-yo tablecloth directions on page 103, step 4). With right sides facing, tack the yo-yos together in a long row; pin and tack the row to the seamed edge of the border and then to the hem of the skirt. As Figure 2 indicates, the yo-yos at each end extend beyond the sides of the skirt.

7. Gather the top of the skirt to 23". Fold the seam allowances on both ends and one long side of the waistband to the back and press. Pin the right side of the waistband's unfolded edge to the wrong side of the skirt's gathered edge and seam together. Fold the waistband to the front of the skirt and edgestitch, covering the previous seam (see Figure 3).

8. Folding each tie lengthwise, sew the cut edges together, leaving one narrow end open. Turn right side out and press. Tuck the open ends of the ties into the open sides of the waistband and topstitch to secure.

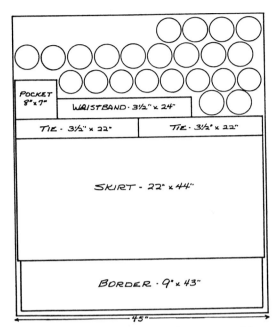

FIGURE 1. Cutting guide for the apron with yo-yos.

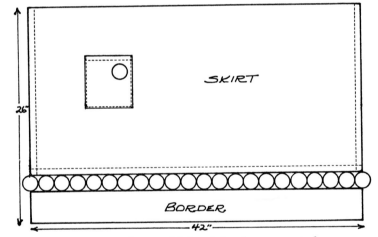

FIGURE 2. Apron skirt and border connected with a row of yo-yos.

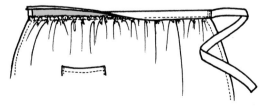

FIGURE 3. Stitching the waistband to the gathered skirt. The ties are attached last.

Casserole Mitts

I have a collection of patchwork potholders, gifts from friends over the years, that I wouldn't dream of using for serious cooking. My workhorse potholders are purchased bargains that I don't care about burning, irreversibly staining, and otherwise abusing. Since my workhorse potholders are an embarrassment, I use my pretty potholders to carry hot dishes when guests are present, but otherwise they stay on the wall.

These casserole mitts, pictured on page 109, fall into the use-only-when-serving category. For that purpose they offer more protection than potholders because, when carrying a hot platter, for example, they protect arms as well as hands.

Occasionally when I'm designing I'll do something for the sake of appearance regardless of the work involved. I like the handsome finish of the binding around these casserole mitts, but it's only fair to warn you that all those angles require finicky attention. If you want your casserole mitts to be less demanding, you could (1) make the end blocks square instead of diagonal at the outside corners, thereby reducing the number of angles you need to miter; or (2) seam the end blocks to the connecting strip with right sides facing (zigzag the seam allowance), binding only the connecting edge in between.

MATERIALS

100% cotton fabrics:

  11" × 11" of a print (fabric A) for the patchwork
  7" × 10" of a coordinating print (fabric B) for the patchwork
  3" × 8" of a coordinating solid (fabric C) for the patchwork
  ½ yard of a solid (fabric D) for the patchwork background and lining
  ½ yard of a print for the binding

Other supplies:

  cotton batting
  safety pins, size 1
  sewing thread that blends with the fabrics being stitched

DIRECTIONS

NOTE: Patterns and dimensions include a ¼" *seam allowance*. Sew with right sides facing, edges matching, unless directed otherwise.

1. Make templates of the square and triangle patterns on page 115.

2. Cut the following:

Fabric	Squares	Triangles	Other
A	12		
B		12	
C	3		
		8	two 6½" × 6½"
D			two 6½" × 11½"
			one 6½" × 28½"

3. As the diagrams in Figure 1 indicate, assemble the three patchwork blocks. First, sew the B and D triangles into squares; next, sew the squares together into rows of three; then sew the rows together, pin-matching the seams that cross. Note that the two end blocks lack corner triangles on one side. Press all seam allowances closed.

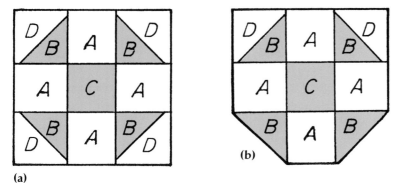

(a)

(b)

FIGURE 1. Piece (a) one center block and (b) two end blocks.

4. Sew the 6½″ × 11½″ pieces of fabric D to opposite sides of the center block. As Figure 2a illustrates, mark these side pieces with a grid of quilting lines 2″ apart. Cut a piece of batting 6½″ × 28½″. With right sides outside, match the pieced top to the lining (6½″ × 28½″ of fabric D) and insert the batting in between. Safety-pin the layers together. Machine-quilt in the ditch following the seams of the patched design and the marked lines.

5. Cut two pieces of batting 6½″ × 6½″. With right sides outside, match the pieced end blocks to linings (6½″ squares of fabric D) and insert batting in between. Trim the corners of the batting and lining to the edge of the top. Safety-pin the layers together and machine-quilt in the ditch following the seams of the patched design.

6. Cut and piece 93″ of binding, 2″ wide, and prepare a doubled binding:

> Bind the straight edges of the end blocks as described below. Pin the end blocks to the lining side of the quilted strip (see Figure 2b); trim the four corners of the quilted strip to match the end blocks; baste the end blocks to the strip with wide zigzag stitching.
>
> With the mitt side up, sew the binding around the banner ¼″ from the matched cut edges, mitering corners and angles. Turning the binding over the edge, blindstitch the binding to the fabric on the other side.

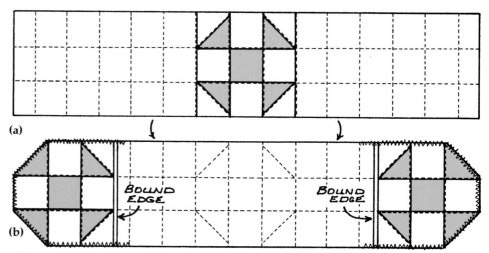

FIGURE 2. (a) 28½″ strip with center block after machine-quilting; (b) quilted end blocks with inner edges bound, machine-basted to the 28½″ strip.

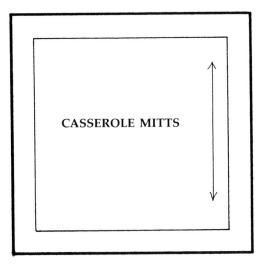

CASSEROLE MITTS

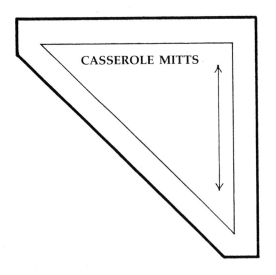

CASSEROLE MITTS

Winter

Outside, colors are at rest. As if to compensate, winter arrives when interiors blaze with holiday brilliance. Wind, snow, ice, shortened days, and long, cold, starry nights keep everyone indoors. After the celebrations that end the year, there's a waiting period, a special time for quilters, that ends when the seasonal cycle begins all over again.

Instructions for the *Winter* panel start on page 17.

The Voices of Children

If the official arrival of winter on December 22nd wasn't mentioned by the forecasters, it would be forgotten in the hustle and bustle of preparing for the holidays to come. Next year, when your television weather person reports that "winter officially begins today," use the announcement as a signal to slow down, hang this banner, and fill your house with the music that celebrates what the festivities are all about.

Banner

"I love it, but I'll never have time to make it!" is no excuse. The "Choristers" banner was planned for speedy machine appliqué and quilting. If you're particularly pressed for time, you can even forgo the quilting; simply line and bind your banner, hang it, and enjoy!

The center figure in my "Choristers" banner is the basic design. The hairstyles and faces of the figures on either side are variations. Using the children in your family as models, for example, you can devise different hairstyles and change expressions by altering the arch of the eyebrows, the opening of the eyes and mouth, and varying the tilt of the head. You may not want to stop at my 12″×30″ trio of choristers, but go on to produce a quartet, a quintet, or even a chorus of little singers.

MATERIALS

100% cotton fabrics:

½ yard of a dark print for the background

6″×36″ of a flesh color for the faces

7½″×10″ of red for the gowns

3½″×30″ of white for the collars

3″×6″ of green for the bows

7″×7″ of three different colors suitable for hair (double this amount if the color is light)

12½″×30½″ of a print or solid for the lining

⅓ yard of a solid for the binding and hanging loops

Other supplies:

tones of blue, brown, and pink six-strand embroidery floss for the facial features

12½″ × 30½″ of batting

safety pins, size 1

sewing thread to match the fabrics being stitched

a 36″ dowel, ½″ in diameter

DIRECTIONS

1. Enlarge the diagram on page 122 and make two copies. Keep one for reference and cut the other apart into patterns for the hair, face, right and left collars, bow, and robe. If desired, design two additional hairstyles and cut hair and face patterns for each.

2. For each of the three blocks, cut the following:

Fabric	Dimensions	Quantity
Background print	12½″ × 10½″	1
Flesh (face)	6″ square	2
Red (gown)	2½″ × 10″	1
White (collar)	2½″ × 3½″	4
Green (bow)	2″ × 3″	1
Hair	7″ square	1*

*2 if the hair color is light

FIGURE 1. Eyebrows embroidered with single stitches, eyelashes with blanket stitch, and mouth with satin stitch.

FIGURE 2. Blanket stitch used to embroider eyelashes.

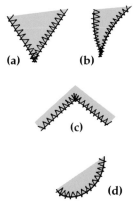

(a)　　**(b)**

(c)

(d)

FIGURE 3. To appliqué corners: (a) satin-stitch up to the corner, pivot with the needle in the background, and continue; or (b) narrow satin-stitch width at the approach to the corner, pivot with the needle in the background, and continue, gradually widening satin-stitch width. Turn an inside angle (c) with stitches radiating from one point, and (d) turn a steep curve with a series of pivots when the needle is in the background.

3. Trace the outline of each face and the facial features onto one 6″ square. With the second square underneath, embroider the features through both layers, as shown in Figure 1. (**HINT:** A 4″ hoop will make embroidering easier.)

Using two or three strands of floss, stitch each eyeline/eyelashes with a blanket stitch (see Figure 2).

Using two or three strands of floss, make each eyebrow with a single stitch.

Using two strands of floss, fill in the mouth with satin stitching. Press facedown on a padded board.

4. Fold each background rectangle in half lengthwise and press a center guideline crease. On the appropriate pieces of fabric, center and trace the outlines of the robe, collar, bow, and hair patterns. Matching centers, machine-appliqué (see Figure 3) each part of the figure to the background in the order shown in Figure 4:

Trim the robe fabric ¼″ from the straight lower edge. Matching the straight edges, center and pin the robe fabric to the background. Straight-stitch over the traced outline. With a small, sharp scissors, trim the excess fabric, cutting up against the side seams and ¼″ away from the seam that matches the edge of the collar. Satin-stitch over the cut edges at the sides, covering the straight stitching.

With a second square underneath, pin-match the curved outlines of the collar, one side at a time, to the matching outlines stitched on the robe. Straight-stitch over the traced collar outlines. Trim the excess fabric, cutting up against the seams at the shoulders and lower collar edges and ¼″ away from the other seams. Satin-stitch over the cut edges at the shoulders and lower collar edges.

Following the same procedures, appliqué the bow and the face, satin-stitching the edges that overlap previous appliqués. Finish with the hair, the only appliqué that will be satin-stitched all around.

Press each finished design face down on a padded board.

5. With right sides facing, edges matching, and a ¼″ seam allowance, sew the three blocks together in a row. Place the appliquéd top (right side up) over the lining (right side down) with the batting in between and safety-pin the layers together. Starting with the center figure, machine-quilt as indicated in Figure 4, outlining each figure's silhouette and face at the edge of the satin stitching and quilting circles in the background. (**HINT:** Use a salad plate and a large dinner plate for circle tracing.) Finish by hand-quilting inside each mouth.

6. Cut and piece 90″ of binding, 2″ wide, and prepare a doubled binding. With the appliquéd side of the banner up, sew the binding around the banner ¼″ from the matched cut edges, mitering the corners. Turning the binding over the banner's edge to the back, blindstitch the binding to the lining.

7. Cut four pieces, each 4″ × 2½″, from the binding fabric. With the right side inside, fold each piece and seam the 4″ sides together. Turn right side out and press. Fold in half and tack the ends of each loop to the top of the banner in back, one at each end and two evenly spaced in between. Insert the dowel through the loops and hang.

FIGURE 4. Appliquéd design with the parts numbered as they are applied and quilting lines indicated.

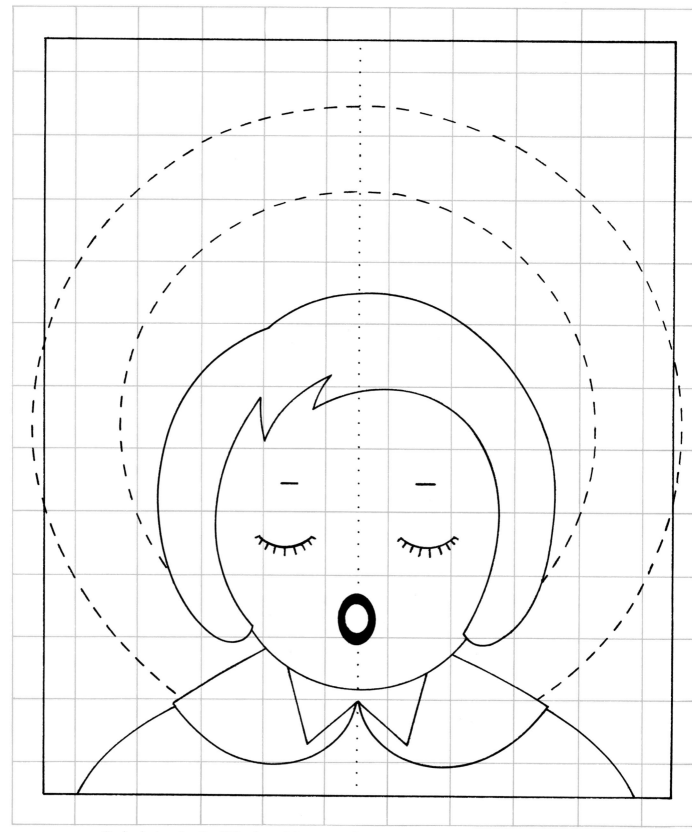

Basic design for the "Choristers" banner, 12″×10″. 1 square = 1 square inch.

Greetings from a Quilter

For those you want to remember with something more personal than a card you buy in a shop, sending a card you've taken the time to make conveys a special message. Sending a card with a memento to keep is even better.

Christmas Cards

These cards with a patchwork ornament serve both purposes. Thanks to that wonderful stuff called transfer web that makes fabric fusible, they're also fun and easy to make.

They're mosaics of cloth fused into designs with an iron. If you start with the nine-patch designs I suggest, I guarantee you'll quickly move on to inventing designs of your own. You may even find yourself, like me, looking for fabric with tiny motifs that you can cut out and frame within the 1″ squares you set into a pattern.

For the neatest results, measure precisely, mark with a pin-sharp pencil, and cut exactly on the line—but always fuse before cutting. You can make cards from a pad of Bristol board, available wherever art supplies are sold.

MATERIALS

white cotton fabric
scraps of cotton prints and solids with patterns and colors suitable for the season
Pellon Wonder-Under™ transfer web
sewing thread for satin-stitched borders
satin ribbon, 1⁄8″ wide
blank cards, 6″ × 4½″, with envelopes

DIRECTIONS

1. Cut a strip of transfer web 3½″ wide and fuse to a strip of white fabric the same size. On the paper backing of the transfer web, center and pencil a strip 3¼″ wide, divided into 3¼″ segments. Cut out these 3¼″ squares. On the fabric side of each square, mark a nine-patch grid of 1″ squares surrounded by a border 1⁄8″ wide (see Figure 1).

2. Fuse strips of transfer web 1¼" wide to strips of colored fabric the same size. On the paper backing, center and pencil a strip 1" wide divided into 1" segments. Cut out these 1" squares. For triangles, cut squares diagonally from corner to corner.

3. Arrange squares and triangles of colored fabric over the nine-patch grid marked on the white background fabric. (See Figure 2 for suggested designs.) Peel off the paper backing on the squares and triangles and fuse the colored design to the background.

4. Peel the paper from the background and fuse to a square of lining fabric the same size. Trim to the edge of the nine-patch design, or leave a narrow border and satin-stitch by machine around the edge.

5. Write your name or initials and the date on the lining side of the ornament. For a hanger, cut and tack the ends of a length of ribbon to one corner or the center of one side. Attach each ornament by its hanger to the front of a card.

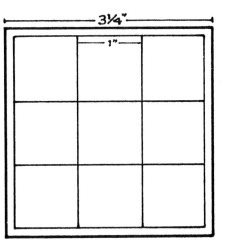

FIGURE 1. Centered nine-patch grid traced on white background fabric.

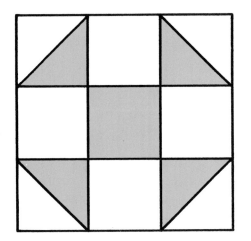

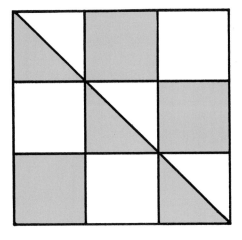

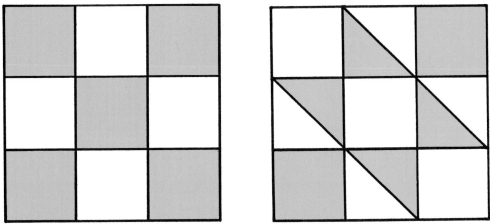

FIGURE 2. Suggested nine-patch designs for fused Christmas card ornaments.

Two for the Tree

Surfaces that shine, glitter, and reflect light are as much a part of Christmas decor as red and green, and for a quilter, Christmas decorations aren't completely satisfying unless they include patchwork as well. These little ornaments satisfy all the requirements. They gleam with metallics and satins pieced together with tiny-figured cotton prints that feature reds and greens in their colorings.

Spin Drops

I like the size of these little elliptical shapes, 4" tip to tip, and their lightness. I like their contrasting textures. I like the way they revolve on their transparent hangers, showing their twisty seaming, catching the light as they turn. And I deeply appreciate their unbreakability.

After you've made a number of spin drops following these basic directions, experiment. Try turning the sections in different directions, combining exotic fabrics, stitching more than two strips together, and embellishing with beads, sequins, lace, ribbon, and tassels.

MATERIALS

  a seasonal cotton print fabric and a metallic fabric (refer to the cutting chart that follows for sizes)
  polyester stuffing
  sewing thread that blends with the fabrics being stitched
  transparent nylon thread for hangers

DIRECTIONS

NOTE: *Pattern and strips include a ¼" seam allowance. Sew with right sides facing and edges matching.*

1. Make a template of the pattern on page 128.
2. Measure and cut the following:

SPIN DROP (cut 4)

Opening—1 side

Opening—1 side

Fabric		Strips			
	Width	Length			
		1 drop	2 drops	3 drops	4 drops
Seasonal cotton print	2¼"	10½"	20"	28½"	37"
Metallic	2¼"	10½"	20"	28½"	37"

3. Machine-stitch the print to the metallic strip along one long edge. Press the seam allowance open. Matching the dotted line on the template to the seamline, trace template outlines on the strip, four for each drop (see Figure 1). Cut out on the traced lines.

4. For each spin drop, machine-stitch two pairs of pattern pieces together along one side, matching the fabrics at the top and bottom.

5. Stitch over the section of seamline reserved for the stuffing opening (see Figure 2). (**HINT:** Keep the openings on the cotton rather than on the metallic end of the drop.) Machine-stitch the two halves of the drop together, leaving the stuffing opening unseamed. Turn the casing right side out.

6. Stuff. Turning the seam allowances inside on the machine stitching, ladder-stitch the opening closed.

7. To make a hanger, run a needle threaded with transparent nylon thread through the tip of the drop and knot the ends together 1½" above the stitch (see Figure 3).

FIGURE 2. Openings stay-stitched before stitching the final seam.

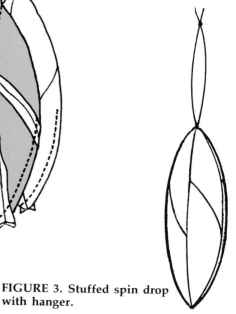

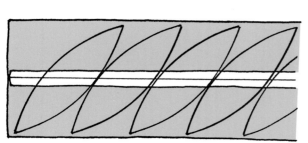

FIGURE 1. Spin drop patterns traced and ready to cut out.

FIGURE 3. Stuffed spin drop with hanger.

128

Mini-Totes

FIGURE 1. Five strip-pieced designs for mini-totes.

As the name suggests, mini-totes, pictured on page 127, are only 4″ square by 1″ deep but, hanging from Christmas greenery, they can be filled with tiny gift-wrapped boxes, dried or artificial flowers and leaves, small toys and candy canes, fluffed tissue paper—or they can be left empty to show off particularly colorful linings. As part of a place setting at a holiday luncheon or dinner, mini-totes could hold real surprises for each guest.

Their patchwork surfaces are quick-pieced from strips, and there's a trick to their construction that makes them easy to assemble. I've suggested simple designs for you to try, but the possibilities are numerous, as I'm sure you'll discover.

MATERIALS

small pieces of coordinating prints and solids—seasonal cotton prints, metallics, and satins—for strip piecing and handles
9½″ × 5½″ of a coordinating print or solid to line each mini-tote
sewing thread to blend with the fabrics being stitched

DIRECTIONS

NOTE: Dimensions include a ¼″ *seam allowance*. Sew with right sides facing, edges matching, unless directed otherwise.

---

1. Measure and cut a paper pattern 9½″ × 5½″.

2. Measure and cut strips of fabric 1½″ wide. Machine-stitch the strips together in rows to make the designs in Figure 1. Start with designs

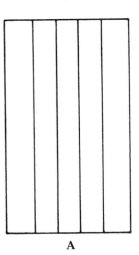

A

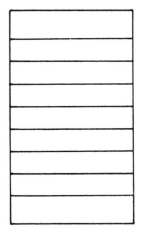

B

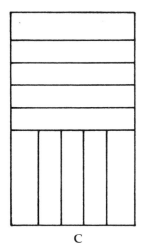

C

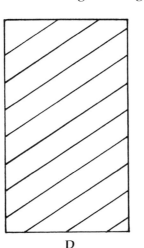

D

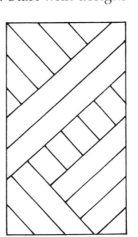

E

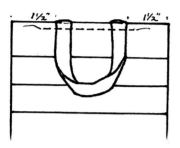

FIGURE 2. Baste a handle to each end of the outside.

A, B, and C, then cut and piece the leftovers to make diagonal designs like D and E. Use the paper pattern to trim the patchwork to the required 9½″ × 5½″ size.

3. Fold two 6″ strips, each 1½″ wide, in half lengthwise and machine-stitch. Turn right side out and press. Machine-baste the handles to the 5½″ sides of the patchwork rectangle (see Figure 2).

4. Machine-stitch the 5½″ sides of the lining to the patchwork, leaving a 2″ opening in the center of one side. Fold the lining in half and the patchwork in half, centering and matching the previous seams, and stitch the sides together (see Figure 3).

5. Box the four corners: fold a corner, centering the side seam; machine-stitch straight across the corner ⅝″ down from the tip, making a seam 1¼″ long (see Figure 4).

6. Turn right side out through the opening. Push the lining down into the inside of the tote. Turning the seam allowances of the opening to the inside, edgestitch next to the fold around the top of the tote, closing the opening in the process. (**HINT:** A cardboard strip fitted inside the bottom of a mini-tote stabilizes the base.)

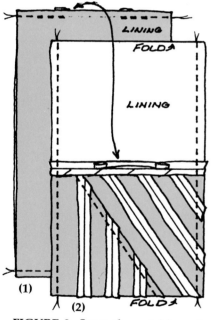

FIGURE 3. Seam the outside and the lining together in two steps.

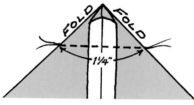

FIGURE 4. Boxing a corner.

Helping Hands

I'm a klutz at buffets. I never seem to have enough hands, particularly for the buffet where I'm expected to cope with a napkin, various utensils, a plate, serving myself from assorted dishes, and a glass of something. To cope with this, one year for a holiday buffet at my house I stitched together a few dozen of these little carriers-with-handles.

Buffet Pockets

If you're planning a buffet, I recommend buffet pockets. Into each put a rolled napkin, a knife, fork, and spoon. Guests pick up one of these buffet pockets, slip the handle over a wrist, and fill their plates and collect a beverage without having to be jugglers.

Because there's no point in making one buffet pocket, the following instructions feature quantity. You'll find that they make up quickly, and even faster if you have a serger for the final finishing.

MATERIALS (for six pockets)

  three coordinating seasonal prints and solids, 100% cotton, 45" wide, for the outside:
  fabric A: a strip 3½" × 45" and one 3" × 45"
  fabric B: a strip 1½" × 45"
  fabric C: a strip 1½" × 45"

  ¼ yard of fabric for the lining

  3 yards of double-fold bias or straight-cut tape, ½" wide, for the handles*

  sewing thread that blends with the fabric being stitched

*To make your own ½" double-fold tape, cut and piece fabric strips 1½" wide; along the length of the strip, fold ¼" seam allowances on each side to the back and press; fold again, matching the previously folded edges, and press.

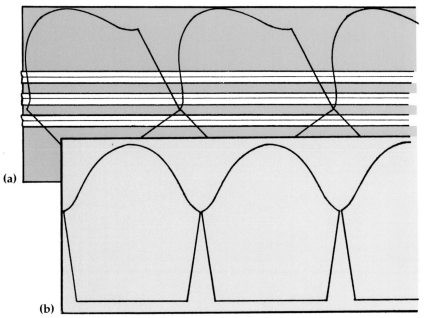

(a)

(b)

FIGURE 1. Pocket outlines traced and ready to cut from (a) the pieced outside and (b) lining fabrics.

DIRECTIONS

NOTE: Pattern and dimensions include a *¼" seam allowance*. Sew with right sides facing, edges matching, unless directed otherwise.

1. Make a template of the pattern on page 134.

2. Machine-stitch the four fabric strips together in the following order: A, 3½"; B, 1½"; C, 1½"; A, 3". Press the seam allowances open. Trace and cut six pockets from the strip-pieced fabric, matching the dotted lines on the template to the seamlines on the fabric.

3. Trace and cut six pocket linings on the straight of the fabric. (See Figure 1.)

4. Topstitch the edges of the folded bias or straight-cut tape together. Divide the 3 yards of tape into six handles, each 18" long.

5. For each buffet pocket, pin one end of a handle to the right side of the lining at X. Sew a strip-pieced outside to the lining around the top curve, catching the handle into the seam. Clip the seam allowance at the inside curves, turn right side out, and press. Fold the pocket in half with the lining outside and sew the straight edges of the pocket together, catching the other end of the handle into the seam as Figure 2 illustrates. Zigzag over the seam allowance. Turn the pocket right side out.

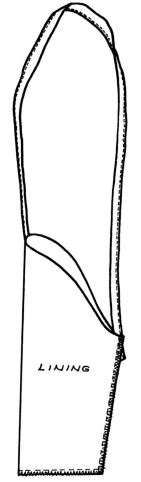

LINING

FIGURE 2. Pocket with handle caught into the seam.

133

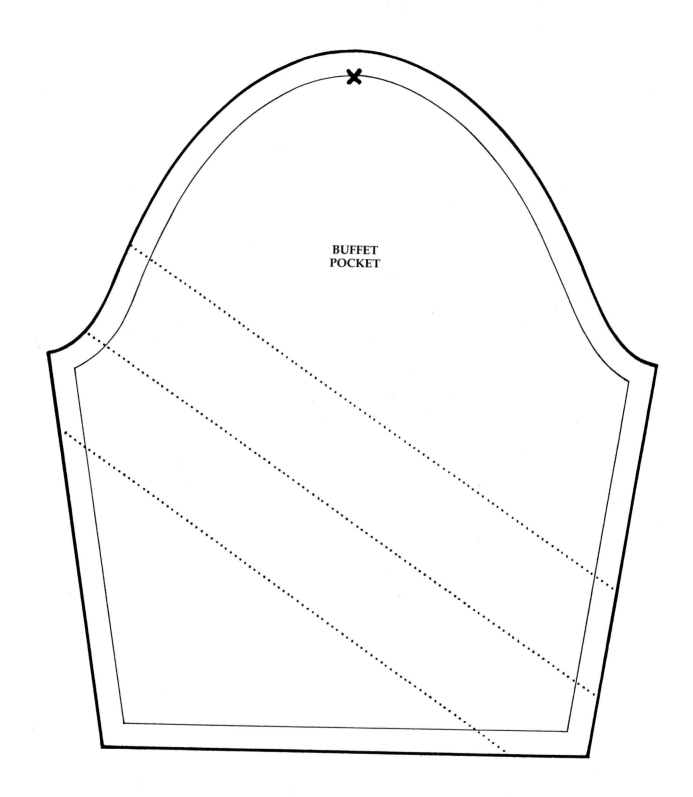

BUFFET
POCKET

134

It's Quilting Time

When the holiday celebrations are over and the decorations are stored for another year, with the house returned to normal and the odd gifts exchanged, a period of waiting for spring to come begins. The cold and the snow keep people indoors, inducing in many a kind of claustrophobia called cabin fever. Impatience and a restless feeling that "the walls are closing in" affects almost everyone except ice skaters and skiers—and quilters. For quilters, it's quilting time.

Tea Cozy

It's time for sitting with a cup of tea in a quiet space and dreaming about all those beautiful quilts just waiting to be made. It's time to plan a quilt around that gorgeous fabric that's been waiting for the perfect design.

There's something reassuring about tea that complements reflection over pictures, patterns, paper and pen, especially tea poured from a pot kept warm under a quilted tea cozy like this one. I colored it red because red signifies warmth and also excitement and passion, qualities shared by quilters when they're involved with quilts.

My tea cozy is pieced into a domed shape that is self-supporting because of the way it's constructed. It's 9½" in diameter at the base. If that's too small for your teapot, you can widen the curving sides of each section accordingly.

MATERIALS

100% cotton fabrics:
   four predominantly red prints and solids for the patchwork:
   9" × 9" of fabric A
   7" × 28" of fabric B
   9" × 26" of fabric C
   7" × 24" of fabric D
   14" × 36" of muslin for the lining
   a strip of black fabric, 2" × 30", for the binding

Other supplies:
   14″ × 36″ of cotton batting
   a half-ball or ball-shaped button
   sewing thread that blends with the fabrics being stitched

DIRECTIONS

NOTE: Patterns and dimensions include a ¼″ *seam allowance*. Sew with right sides facing, edges matching, unless directed otherwise.

---

1. Make templates of the patterns on page 138.
2. Cut the following:

Fabric	Pattern	Quantity
A	#1	6
B	#2	6 and 6*
C	#3	6
D	#4	6 and 6*

*with the template reversed

Mark each fabric pattern piece with ▼ 's as the templates indicate.

3. Pressing the seam allowances closed after each step, piece the six patchwork sections, matching all ▼ 's. For each section:

Start by sewing #1 to #2 (see Figure 1a), then seam #3 to a reversed #2 (see Figure 1b).

Sew these combinations together, matching the central seam (see Figure 1c).

Finish with a #4 seamed to each lower diagonal side (see Figure 1d).

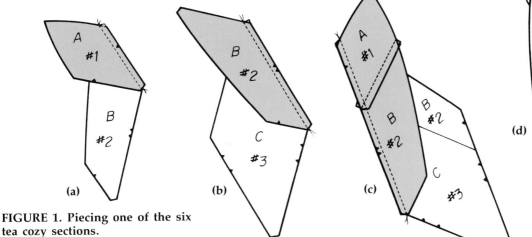

FIGURE 1. Piecing one of the six tea cozy sections.

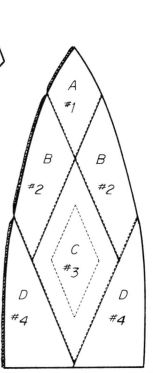

FIGURE 2. A machine-quilted tea cozy section.

4. Spread the batting over the lining. Pin the pieced sections, arranged next to each other, on top. Cut a batting and lining to the exact size of each section. As Figure 2 illustrates, machine-quilt each section, following the seamlines in the ditch and quilting a diamond ⅝" inside the seam of piece #3. (**Hint:** Sew next to the edge of masking tape ⅝" wide.)

5. Trim 1" of the batting out of the tip of each section. Stitching through all layers and matching the piecing seams, pin and sew a curving side of two sections together. With a wide but close zigzag, stitch over the seam allowance. Add a third section; zigzag over the seam allowance. Sew the remaining three sections together in the same manner. Then straight-stitch and zigzag the two halves of the tea cozy together, matching the piecing seams.

6. Fold the binding in half lengthwise, right side outside, and press. With the patchwork side of the tea cozy up, sew the doubled binding around the base ¼" from the matched cut edges. Turning the binding over the cozy's edge to the back, blindstitch the binding to the lining.

7. Attach a button to the peak of the tea cozy.

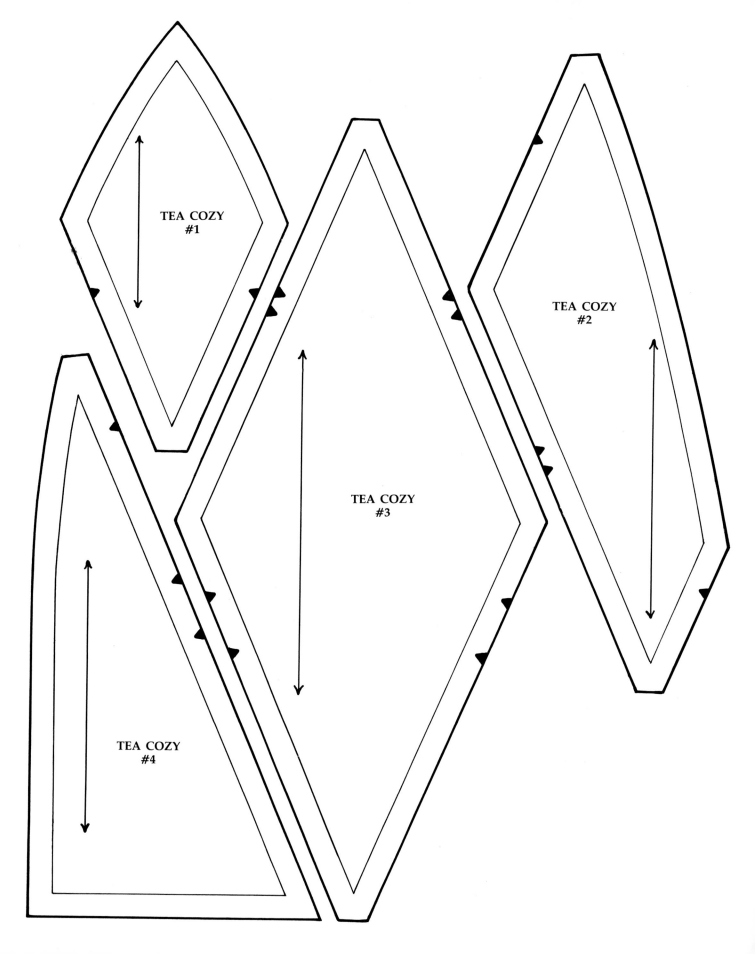

Comforter

This comforter will keep the drafts away while you're quilting during the cabin-fever months. It's a variation of an old pattern called Wild Goose Chase that I call "Wild Goose Memories." My example has a column of paired geese for each season of the year cut from eighty-eight of the prints and solids I used in the projects for this book. In the years to come when I wrap myself in its soft and cozy warmth, I'll remember the time I worked on *Seasonal Patchwork and Quilting,* represented by all those pieces of cloth.

Memories are essential ingredients to sew into your personal comforter. Use scraps left over from past projects. Ask your quilting friends for cutaways from quilts you admire. You can cut and piece the top all at once or make "Wild Goose Memories" an extended work-in-progress, stitching the units as you collect memorable fabrics.

The simplicity of the wild goose pattern conceals a challenge—the points of all those triangles. To interpret the pattern correctly, those points should be sharply defined and the units should fly in perfect alignment horizontally as well as vertically. That requires precision— precise, consistent, unwavering cutting and seaming. (**HINT:** Just in case, the ties at the tips of the "wings" will conceal little inaccuracies!)

"Wild Goose Memories" is 68″ × 52″ when finished. Lining it with flannel will keep it from slipping off your lap.

MATERIALS

an assortment of 100% cotton prints and solids for the geese

2¼ yards of black 100% cotton, 45″ wide, for the background

one flannel sheet, single bed size, or 3½ yards of 100% cotton flannel, 45″ wide

1½ yards of black 100% cotton, 45″ wide, for the binding

hi-loft batting

safety pins, size 1

6 skeins or cards of white embroidery floss for the ties

black sewing thread

DIRECTIONS

NOTE: Patterns and dimensions include a *¼″ seam allowance.* Sew with right sides facing, edges matching, unless directed otherwise.

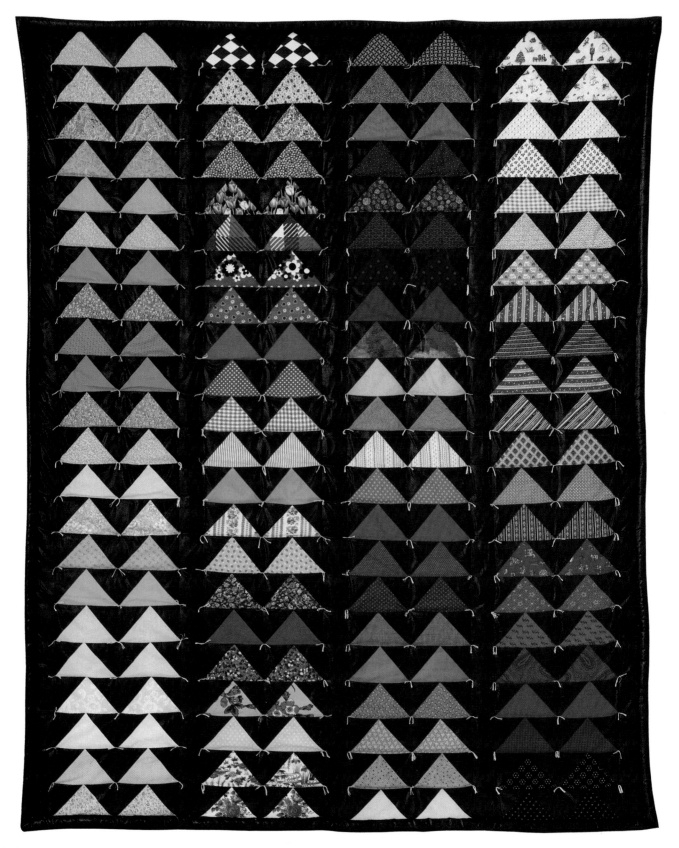

1. Make templates of the patterns on page 143.

2. Cut the following:

Fabric	Pattern	Quantity	Size
Assorted prints and solids	#1	176	
		5	*2½″ × 66½″*
Black	#1	88	
	#2	176**	

*Cut these strips before cutting the patterns.
**If the fabric has a right and a wrong side, cut eighty-eight with the pattern reversed.

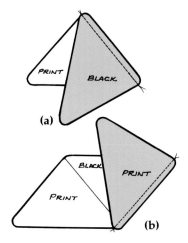
(a)

(b)

3. Pressing the seam allowances closed over the black triangles after each seam, piece the four wild goose strips (see Figure 1):

Make eighty-eight double triangle units as Figure 1a illustrates.

Arrange the eighty-eight double triangle units into four rows, each twenty-two units long, and seam together. Each row should finish 66½″ long.

4. As the diagram on page 142 indicates, assemble the four wild goose rows with black strips 66½″ × 2½″ in between and at the sides. Press these seam allowances closed over the strips.

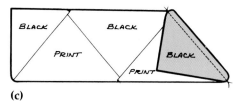
(c)

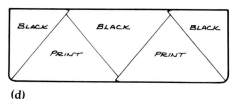
(d)

FIGURE 1. To assemble a wild goose unit: (a) sew a black to a print triangle; (b) stitch a second print to the black triangle; (c) seam the black corner triangles to the print triangles; (d) the finished unit.

5. Cut lining and batting 71″ × 55″, about 2″ larger all around than the top (if you are using yardage instead of a sheet, cut 3½ yards in half and seam together before trimming to size). Spread the lining face down on a large surface, smooth the batting over the lining, and center the wild goose top over the batting. Safety-pin the layers together, pinning alternate rows of goose triangles through their centers.

6. Starting in the center of the comforter and working out to the edges, tie the layers together. Make a tie at the base or wing corners of every goose triangle:

Thread a large-eyed needle with embroidery floss. Push the needle *straight* down through all layers, bringing it out underneath. Leave a 3″ tail on top. Reinserting the needle into the lining no more than ¼″ away from the point where the thread emerged, push the needle *straight* back up through all layers, bringing it out on top. Repeat. Tie the ends of the floss together in a tight square knot (see Figure 2) and cut ½″ from the knot, leaving the tails of the floss to fray out.

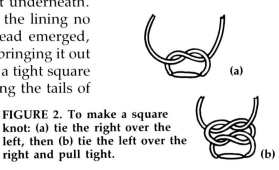
(a)

(b)

FIGURE 2. To make a square knot: (a) tie the right over the left, then (b) tie the left over the right and pull tight.

141

Layout of the 68″ × 52″ "Wild Goose Memories" comforter.

1 square = 8 square inches.

7. Cut and piece 7 yards of binding, 5″ wide, and prepare a doubled binding. To control the edge of the top, baste it through the batting to the lining, sewing within the ¼″ seam allowance. Matching the cut edges of the binding to the edge of the top, sew the doubled binding around the quilt with a ¼″ seam allowance, mitering the corners. (**Hint**: Flatten the puffy batting to the right of the seam with a short, rigid ruler.) Trim the batting and lining 1⅛″ from the seam. Turning the binding over the comforter's edge to the back, blindstitch the binding to the lining. For a puffy binding, insert narrow strips of batting under the binding as you proceed.

8. Attach a label with your name and the date to one corner of the lining.

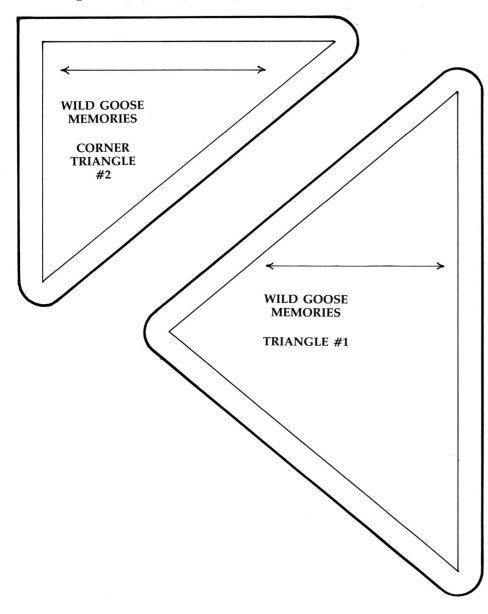

WILD GOOSE
MEMORIES

CORNER
TRIANGLE
#2

WILD GOOSE
MEMORIES

TRIANGLE #1

Index

All of us at Meredith® Press are dedicated to offering you, our customer, the best books we can create. We are particularly concerned that all of the instructions for making projects are clear and accurate. Please address your correspondence to Customer Service Department, Meredith® Press, Meredith Corporation, 150 East 52nd Street, New York, NY 10022.

Seasonal Patchwork & Quilting is the fourth in a series of patchwork and quilting books. If you would like the first three books in the series, *Country Patchwork & Quilting*, *Romantic Patchwork & Quilting*, and *Classic Patchwork & Quilting*, please write to Better Homes and Gardens Books, P.O. Box 10670, Des Moines, Iowa 50336, or call 1-800-678-2665.